Money

Guide to Investing
in the Stockmarket

OTHER TITLES IN THIS SERIES INCLUDE

Moneywise Guide to Your Pension

Moneywise Guide to Tax

Moneywise Guide to Planning Your Finances

Moneywise

Guide to Investing in the Stockmarket

CHRISTINE STOPP

RD Publications Ltd · London

in association with

Prentice Hall Europe

London   New York   Toronto   Sydney   Tokyo   Singapore   Madrid
Mexico City   Munich   Paris

First published 1998 by
Prentice Hall Europe
Campus 400, Maylands Avenue
Hemel Hempstead
Hertfordshire HP2 7EZ
A division of
Simon & Schuster International Group

Every possible care has been taken to ensure the accuracy of the information
in this book, but no responsibility can be accepted for the consequences
of actions based on the advice contained therein. Readers are encouraged
to take relevant professional advice based on personal circumstances.

Editorial:
Brown Packaging Books Ltd
Bradley's Close
74–77 White Lion Street
London N1 9PF

Design:
Kingfisher Design, London N2 9NR

Printed and bound in Great Britain by:
T.J. International Ltd, Padstow

Library of Congress Cataloging-in-Publication Data

Available from the publisher

British Library Cataloguing in Publication Data

A catalogue record for this book is available from the British Library

ISBN: 0-13-911033-X

1 2 3 4 5   02 01 00 99 98

Contents

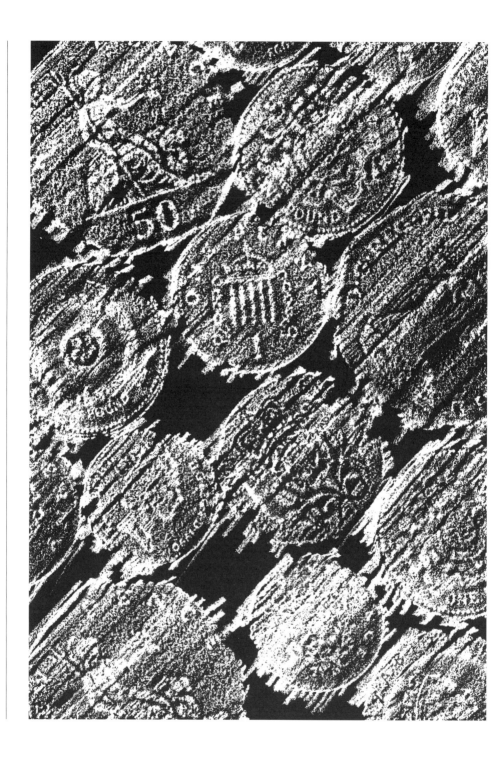

About the **Money**wise
Ask the Professionals
panel...

THROUGHOUT THIS BOOK you will find comments and explanations from members of the *Moneywise* Ask the Professionals panel. The members are authorised professional advisers specialising in different areas of financial planning who answer *Moneywise* readers' letters every month. The panel aims to answer any financial queries. The service is free and using it puts you under no obligation whatsoever.

For advice write to:
'Ask the Professionals'
Moneywise
11 Westferry Circus
Canary Wharf
London E14 4HE

JANET ADAM is a tax partner at chartered accountants BDO Stoy Hayward, based in Manchester

WALTER AVRILI is operations director at independent mortgage advisers John Charcol in London

BRIAN DENNEHY is an independent financial adviser and managing director of Dennehy, Weller & Co in Kent

KEAN SEAGER is an independent financial adviser and managing director of Whitechurch Securities in Bristol

KEITH SANHAM is an independent financial adviser at Fairmount Trust Plc, based in Leatherhead, Surrey

REBEKAH KEAREY is an independent financial adviser and a partner at Roundhill Financial Management in Brighton.

Preface

You've just got past the biggest difficulty most people face with their finances. You've got past page 1 – and you're still reading. With most financial literature, that's unusual. Fear, fatigue or frustration would normally have set in by now – caused by figures, jargon, cf paragraph C sub-section  three... and more figures. That's why most financial books go unread, why most bank statements go unopened... why most self-assessment tax-returns go back late.

But money doesn't have to be that difficult. If you flick through some of these pages, you'll be looking at flowcharts that show your financial choices in simple terms. And with a *Moneywise* publication, that's not unusual. *Moneywise* has always set out to make money make sense – key facts and figures, plain English, clear headings and action points. That's why *Moneywise* is Britain's best-read personal finance magazine... and probably why you opened this book.

And now that you've started, you'll find it gets easier. As you read more pages of these *Moneywise* guides, you'll get to know more about financial planning, pensions, tax and stockmarket investments. You'll find that this knowledge really does give you power. You'll know what to ask, what to look for and what to expect when you deal with financial companies. You may start by following our action points but go on to work out your own!

All the action points and flowcharts in our guides have been put together with this aim in mind. We asked leading independent financial advisers (IFAs) and *Moneywise*'s award-winning financial journalists to provide you with up-to-date practical advice – not textbook tax book theory.

It's all just over the page. So get past this preface and get to the advice you need. But if you're still standing in the bookshop reading this, go via the cash desk – you'll find this is an investment that will really pay off.

Matthew Vincent

Matthew Vincent
Editor
Moneywise

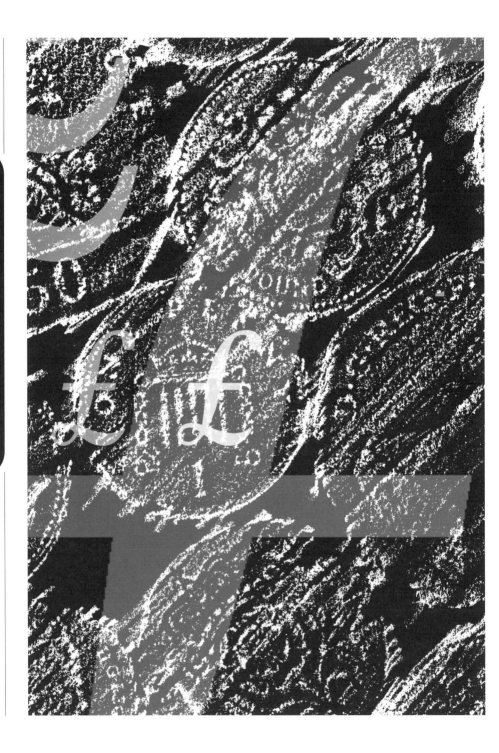

1
Why invest in the stockmarket?

The stockmarket is of great importance to investors. More than that, it is an essential part of investing to provide for long-term growth and a comfortable retirement for the majority of the population. It is also a fascinating subject to find out about, whether as a way of increasing your wealth or as a hobby with a bit of built-in excitement.

Independent financial adviser and *Moneywise* Ask the Professionals panellist Brian Dennehy says:

"Investing in the stockmarket is exciting because making money is exciting and most of the time people will make money investing! And learning is exciting – you will never stop learning if you take an interest in the stockmarket."

You don't have to be very wealthy to invest in the stockmarket. Fortunes can be lost through unwise and speculative investment in shares, but, as we shall see in Chapter 9, even very small investors with not much scope for risk can enjoy some of the thrills and spills of the stockmarket index without major damage to their lifestyle.

The fact is, you are probably a stockmarket investor already, whether you know it or not. Look at the list of investments on page 14 and put a tick in the box if you own any of these.

If you have ticked any of the boxes, then more or less directly you are already investing in the stockmarket. For example, your company pension scheme and your with-profits policy alike give an investment return which is at least partly derived from shares or other securities. Your future and that of the stockmarket are already inextricably linked.

WHY IS THE STOCKMARKET SO IMPORTANT?

There is one overwhelming reason for investing in the stockmarket: it has a long history of providing inflation-beating investment growth. This may not sound earth-shattering, but despite the fact that inflation has been low for the past few years, it is constantly eat-

Are you a stockmarket investor?

TICK THE BOXES IF YOU HOLD ...		Employee share options	☐
Gilts (government stocks)	☐	Company pension scheme	☐
PEPs	☐	Corporate bond PEP	☐
With-profits endowment policy	☐	Unit trusts	☐
Privatisation issue shares	☐	Investment trusts	☐
Personal pension plan	☐	Unit-linked life policy	☐

ing away at your wealth. The box on page 15 shows how inflation at a steady rate reduces the value of your money. After 15 years at 3% your £100 will be worth only £65. If inflation averaged 5%, the same amount would be worth £49. In fact, inflation has averaged 4·6% over the last 15 years.

For your assets to hold their value they must grow faster than the Retail Price Index. This will be especially important in your retirement. The stockmarket, above all other forms of investment, has a strong record of making the value of investors' money grow faster than inflation – so although it carries the risk that share prices might fall, few investors can afford to ignore it.

Each year stockbrokers Barclays de Zoete Wedd (BZW) publish a survey of growth in share prices compared to government stocks (gilts) and other forms of investment. The table on page 16 shows the results: if you had invested £100 in shares in December 1945, it would have been worth £25,017 on 31 December 1996. A similar investment in a building society share account would have grown to £1,063 since 1945. This is without counting the effect of inflation. In real terms (that is, after

EXAMPLE
A major life insurance company decided to launch a range of unit trusts. It conducted extensive research among investors, asking them whether they held stock-market investments. Most said no. But when groups of people with no share invest-ments were picked for detailed interviews, researchers found that many held BT shares. They had not realised that holding shares made them stockmarket investors!

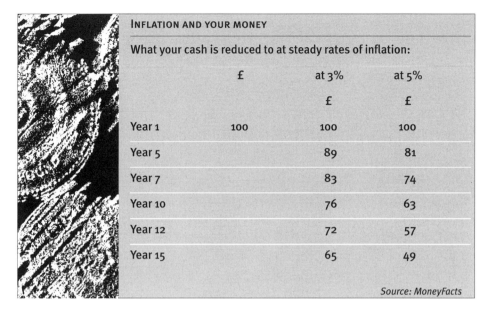

INFLATION AND YOUR MONEY

What your cash is reduced to at steady rates of inflation:

	£	at 3%	at 5%
		£	£
Year 1	100	100	100
Year 5		89	81
Year 7		83	74
Year 10		76	63
Year 12		72	57
Year 15		65	49

Source: MoneyFacts

allowing for inflation) the share price investment would be worth £1,187 and the building society investment would have fallen to £50. So the real value of your money would have grown more than ten-fold in shares – or have been halved in the building society.

BUT IS IT FUN?

Looked at this way, the stockmarket seems a very serious business, but many people are attracted to it because, like a rollercoaster, it can offer plenty of excitement.

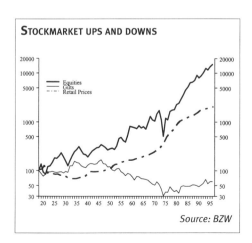

STOCKMARKET UPS AND DOWNS

Equities
Gilts
Retail Prices

Source: BZW

The graph shows how the share market has performed since 1920. The ups and downs – some of them very dramatic – do not mask the fact that the overall trend is upward. The longer-term tendency for markets to beat inflation is also clear, though you can see that over some shorter periods inflation would have won the battle.

From 1970 to 1976, a period which included one of the market's great crashes, the investor would

15

HOW YOUR MONEY HAS GROWN (OR HAS IT?)

Returns on a £100 investment since December 1945

	Equities (ie stockmarket shares)		Building society share account	
	Value £	After inflation £	Value £	After inflation £
1945	100	100	100	100
1960	395	233	154	91
1975	944	187	321	64
1990	10,882	614	899	51
1996	25,017	1,187	1,063	50

Source: BZW Securities — Equity & Building Society share funds

have seen his or her assets rocket then plunge again, ending up back around its starting value. Inflation, meanwhile, rose steadily and it was not until the 1980s that the stockmarket investor caught up.

Sometimes, investing is a particular stock can really pay off (see chart on page 17). But share prices can fall as well as rise, and in extreme cases the company can go bust and you can lose your entire investment. There are ways of reducing the level of risk you are taking on. First you should decide on your personal risk profile.

WHERE ARE YOU ON THE RISK SPECTRUM?

See where your investment needs fit on the risk graph (page 18). You may find that some of your answers suggest a high-risk, others a low-risk profile. If in doubt, err on the side of caution.

For example although the couple in the example to the right dislike the idea of risk, their stockbroker recommends some stockmarket investment to help their money keep pace with inflation. They decide on unit

EXAMPLE
A married couple in their fifties have savings of £75,000 held in deposit accounts. They have full pension provision based on the husband's earnings but want to increase the return on their money to cover possible long-term care needs, and to be able to help their children financially.

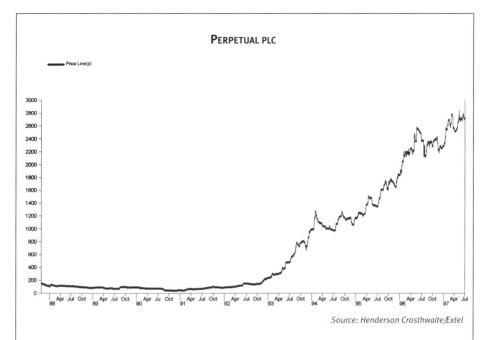

PERPETUAL PLC

— Price Line(p)

Source: Henderson Crosthwaite/Extel

EXAMPLE: PERPETUAL – A PROFITABLE CHOICE

Investors who manage to harness an upswing in an individual stock can do very well. In the early 1990s an investor who prided herself on knowing a bit about unit trusts took out a PEP with Perpetual fund managers. Her PEP did well. She decided to go one step further and buy £1,000 of shares in the management group itself. She bought the stock at 70p in mid 1992. By the end of 1996, following a stretch of award-winning performance by the group, Perpetual's share price had reached £20. Her £1,000 investment was now worth £28,571.

trusts and investment trusts for the bulk of the cash, transferring as much as possible each year into tax-free PEPs. Their choice includes some blue chip shares held through a single company PEP.

SHOULD YOU INVEST IN THE STOCKMARKET?

If you know how much risk you can tolerate, and you take steps to control risk within your investment portfolio, a stockmarket investment in some form will probably be beneficial. There are a few categories of people for whom it is unlikely to be suitable: very elderly investors, those struggling to make ends meet and those who have little cash to invest. The flowchart on page 20 is a guide to whether or not the stockmarket is for you.

Where are you on the risk spectrum?

(For suggestions on portfolios in each category, see Chapter 3)	Risk averse	Medium-risk profile	High-risk profile
YOUR AGE			
○ under 35		▬▬▬▬▬	▬▬▬▬▬
○ 35–50		▬▬▬	
○ 50–65	▬▬▬▬▬	▬▬▬	
○ 65 plus	▬▬▬		
YOUR INVESTMENT IS			
○ a small part of your total assets		▬▬▬▬▬	▬▬▬▬
○ a large part of your total assets	▬▬		
○ an unexpected cash windfall which you can afford to lose			▬▬▬
YOU ALREADY HAVE			
○ few savings	▬▬▬		
○ some savings	▬▬▬▬		
○ a substantial spread of savings and investments		▬▬▬▬▬	▬▬▬
YOU WANT TO INVEST FOR			
○ the long term (5–10 years plus)		▬▬▬▬▬	▬▬▬
○ less than five years	▬▬		
○ maximum growth and a fast turnaround			▬▬▬
YOUR INVESTMENT OBJECTIVES			
○ you need specific returns in a defined period (eg house deposit or school fees)	▬▬▬		
○ you just want to build a nest egg long term		▬▬▬▬▬	▬▬▬
○ income	▬▬▬▬▬	▬▬	
○ you will need instant short-term access to your cash	▬▬▬		
YOUR APPROACH TO RISK			
○ you don't like the idea of risk at all	▬▬▬		
○ you don't like risk, but you do need inflation-beating growth	▬▬▬▬▬	▬▬	
○ you accept there are risks attached to share investment, but feel they are acceptable if properly managed		▬▬▬▬▬	▬▬▬
○ you want maximum returns and will accept high risks to get them			▬▬▬

Independent financial adviser and *Moneywise* Ask the Professionals panellist Brian Dennehy says:

"Imagine the sum you are investing. Now imagine the value has fallen 20% in a few days. How will you react? Will you be depressed and looking for someone else to blame? If so don't put your money into risky investments. Alternatively reduce the amount you were considering investing, perhaps with monthly contributions rather than a lump sum. And imagine it's ten years on and your money is still invested. The value is still less than your original investment and at times has fallen by more than 50%. If you couldn't cope with this the advice above applies."

SHOULD YOU INVEST DIRECTLY OR THROUGH FUNDS?

This book covers all types of stockmarket investment. When talking about the stockmarket, most people think about shares. We shall be covering share investment in detail.

However, another way to invest in the stockmarket is through investment funds, such as unit trusts and investment trusts. These are large, professionally managed pools of investment holdings. A fund might hold shares in a hundred or more companies, as well as in different world markets. The investor's shares or units in the fund represent a percentage of the pooled holding, so that even a £500 investment could give you the benefit of a very wide range of stocks.

Funds have a lot of advantages for private investors. The flowchart on page 21 will help you choose between funds and direct share investments.

SHOULD YOU INVEST IN PEPs?

With any type of investment an important consideration is tax. Personal equity plans (PEPs) were designed to encourage private investors into the stockmarket. If you hold a PEP all your returns are free of tax. The flowchart on page 22 will help you decide whether PEPs are for you.

SHOULD YOU GO IT ALONE OR TAKE ADVICE?

For some, investment is a fascinating hobby. Others, while wanting to have their financial affairs in order and to make proper provision for their future, are not interested in the day-to-day workings of the stockmarket, or don't have time to make their own decisions. Should you rely on your own knowledge, or take advice? The flowchart on page 23 takes you through the issues.

Should you invest in the stockmarket?

Have you already got:
- emergency cash
- life cover
- pension arrangements

Yes / **No** → These are essentials – you should have all three before considering direct stockmarket investment.

Do you already have some savings/investments?

Yes / **No**

Do you want long-term growth?

Would the risk of falling prices keep you awake at night?

Yes / **No**

Do you have:
- £10,000 plus to invest?
- less than £10,000 to invest?

A lower risk investment would be better for you.

Though you are wary of risk, you need stockmarket growth. See **Reducing risk** in Chapter 3.

Do you want a short-term investment which may be called upon within 5 years?

If the money is wanted for a specific purpose within 5 years, the stockmarket is too risky.

Proceed to **Building Your Portfolio** in Chapter 3.

Do you want some excitement with a bit of spare cash?

Is this money you could afford to lose?

Yes / **No**

Go ahead – and good luck!

You should have some lower risk savings before you consider the stockmarket.

Do you want income?

See the **Income flowchart** on page 89.

Should you invest directly or through funds?

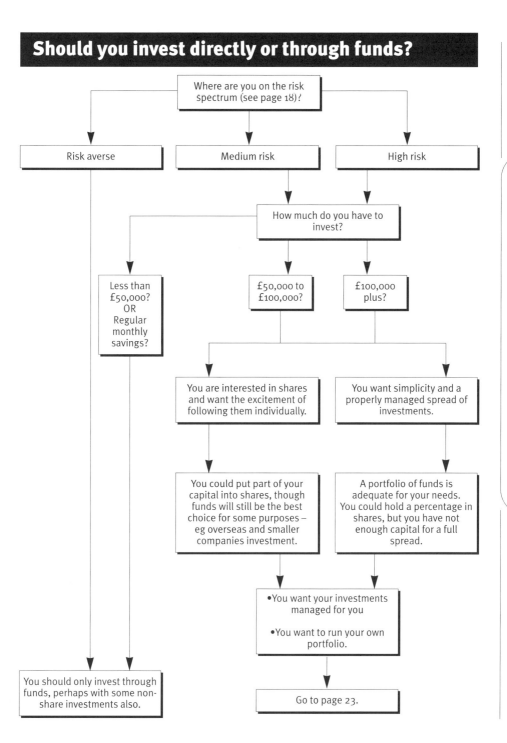

Where are you on the risk spectrum (see page 18)?

Risk averse | Medium risk | High risk

How much do you have to invest?

Less than £50,000?
OR
Regular monthly savings?

£50,000 to £100,000?

£100,000 plus?

You are interested in shares and want the excitement of following them individually.

You want simplicity and a properly managed spread of investments.

You could put part of your capital into shares, though funds will still be the best choice for some purposes – eg overseas and smaller companies investment.

A portfolio of funds is adequate for your needs. You could hold a percentage in shares, but you have not enough capital for a full spread.

• You want your investments managed for you

• You want to run your own portfolio.

You should only invest through funds, perhaps with some non-share investments also.

Go to page 23.

WHY INVEST IN THE STOCKMARKET?

21

Should you invest in PEPs?

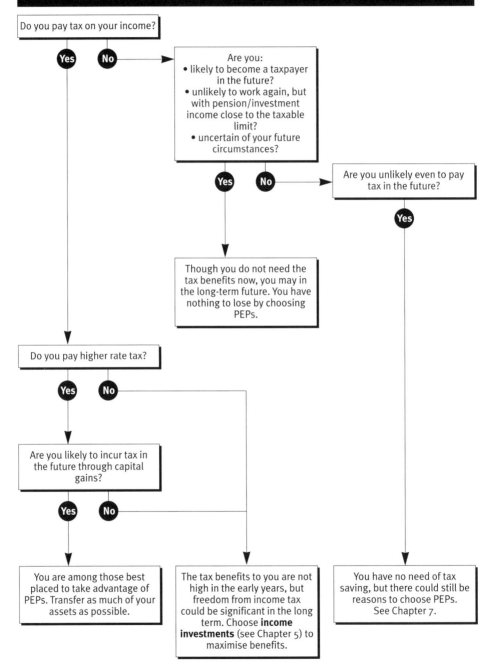

Do you pay tax on your income?

Yes **No**

Are you:
• likely to become a taxpayer in the future?
• unlikely to work again, but with pension/investment income close to the taxable limit?
• uncertain of your future circumstances?

Yes **No**

Are you unlikely even to pay tax in the future?

Yes

Though you do not need the tax benefits now, you may in the long-term future. You have nothing to lose by choosing PEPs.

Do you pay higher rate tax?

Yes **No**

Are you likely to incur tax in the future through capital gains?

Yes **No**

You are among those best placed to take advantage of PEPs. Transfer as much of your assets as possible.

The tax benefits to you are not high in the early years, but freedom from income tax could be significant in the long term. Choose **income investments** (see Chapter 5) to maximise benefits.

You have no need of tax saving, but there could still be reasons to choose PEPs. See Chapter 7.

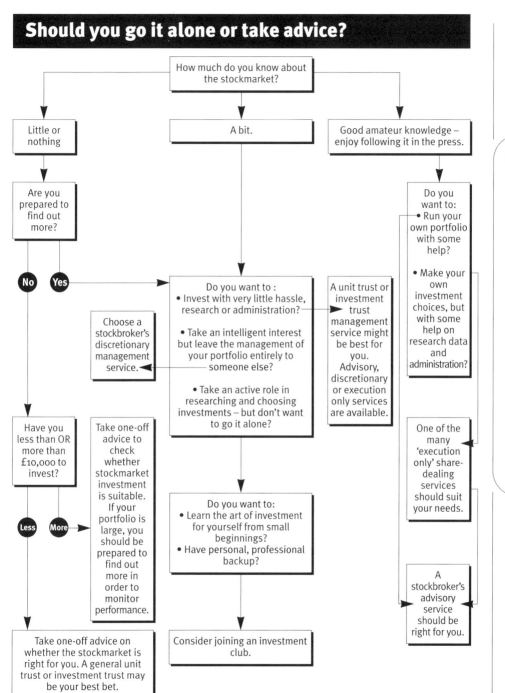

Should you go it alone or take advice?

How much do you know about the stockmarket?

Little or nothing

A bit.

Good amateur knowledge – enjoy following it in the press.

Are you prepared to find out more?

No **Yes**

Do you want to:
• Run your own portfolio with some help?

• Make your own investment choices, but with some help on research data and administration?

Choose a stockbroker's discretionary management service.

Do you want to :
• Invest with very little hassle, research or administration?

• Take an intelligent interest but leave the management of your portfolio entirely to someone else?

• Take an active role in researching and choosing investments – but don't want to go it alone?

A unit trust or investment trust management service might be best for you. Advisory, discretionary or execution only services are available.

Have you less than OR more than £10,000 to invest?

Take one-off advice to check whether stockmarket investment is suitable. If your portfolio is large, you should be prepared to find out more in order to monitor performance.

One of the many 'execution only' share-dealing services should suit your needs.

Less **More**

Do you want to:
• Learn the art of investment for yourself from small beginnings?
• Have personal, professional backup?

A stockbroker's advisory service should be right for you.

Take one-off advice on whether the stockmarket is right for you. A general unit trust or investment trust may be your best bet.

Consider joining an investment club.

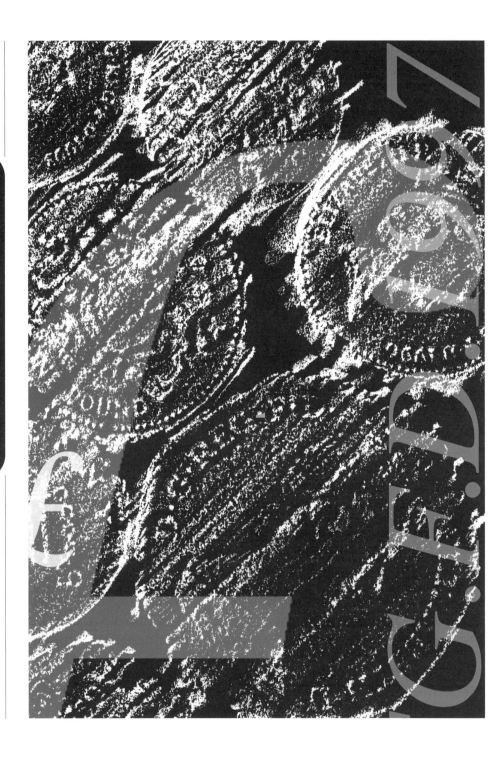

2
How the stockmarket works

A stockmarket is an arena for dealing in the shares of companies. Stockmarkets are recognised as an effective way of raising money for commercial enterprise, and at the same time providing an investment for individuals and institutions willing to put up the money.

As we saw in Chapter 1, stockmarkets carry an inherent risk but also a good chance of long-term reward.

Many countries have stockmarkets, and today developing countries are in the process of establishing stock exchanges. The table on page 26 shows the estimated sizes of most of the major world markets in terms of market capitalisation, which is calculated by the number of shares in issue multiplied by the share price. The USA, Japan and the UK stand out as the three biggest individual markets; the London market alone is valued at over £1,000bn.

HOW IT STARTED

The concept of the joint stock company, which is at the heart of stockmarkets, first appeared in London in 1553. The company concerned was set up, following advice from explorer Sebastian Cabot, to find a north-east passage to China for trading purposes. Only one of his three ships survived, and ended up being feted at the court of Czar Ivan the Terrible, who was keen to trade.

The resulting Muscovy Company established a principle: it was owned by those who had put up the original capital, but managed separately by a governor appointed by the shareholders. Its shares could be traded freely.

At the end of the 17th century trading in gilts stocks (see Chapter 8) was also established as a way of raising money for government. Trading grew rapidly and by 1697 the first legislation appeared in order to control the brokers and stockjobbers.

World markets

Estimated total market capitalisations in US$m at 30.6.97

	US$M		US$M
AUSTRIA	35,693	SWEDEN	272,006
BELGIUM	131,400	SWITZERLAND	522,477
DENMARK	80,679	UNITED KINGDOM	1,870,353
FINLAND	75,063	AUSTRALIA	327,316
FRANCE	640,091	HONG KONG	427,347
GERMANY	765,703	JAPAN	3,312,277
IRELAND	40,059	MALAYSIA	281,987
ITALY	286,033	NEW ZEALAND	40,273
NETHERLANDS	462,514	SINGAPORE	134,994
NORWAY	62,868	CANADA	520,553
SPAIN	260,924	USA	8,919,909

Source: Morgan Stanley Capital International

Brokers were people who traded in the market on behalf of client investors. Jobbers operated in the market on their own account, dealing only with brokers but not with the public directly. The system of brokers and jobbers was only formalised in 1908, but it lasted until the major market reform of the 1980s.

In the 18th century dealing firms emerged, running their businesses from coffee houses in the City of London. By the 1760s these businesses had become more formal and in 1773 the Stock Exchange itself was established.

The London Stock Exchange continued to grow and develop and is now of enormous importance to investors of all kinds, whether through direct investment or, as we saw in Chapter 1, through a variety of means such as pensions. Though it has, on the whole, a good record for growth, it has not been without its disasters.

One of the most famous Stock Exchange crashes was the South Sea Bubble in the 1720s, when a government company set up to trade in South America and the Pacific attracted wild speculation. The company collapsed, and many investors were ruined.

'Boom and bust' conditions are not unknown today. The runaway (so-called 'bull') market of the 1980s crashed in 1987. Though some stocks rapidly lost a third of their value, for the long-term investor even this looks like a blip on the graph of overall market growth. In Chapter 3 we look at risk and different strategies for handling it.

THE MARKET TODAY

In 1986 there was major reform of the Stock Exchange, known as 'Big Bang'. The ownership rules were changed, allowing foreign organisations to own stockbroking firms; minimum scales of commission were abolished, opening the way for cut-price share dealing; and the separation between brokers and jobbers ended. All firms are now broker/dealers. There are 33 registered as market makers, who are committed to making firm buying and selling prices at any time in a particular range of UK shares. There are 44 market makers handling international shares listed on the market.

The Stock Exchange has grown very fast since Big Bang. At the end of 1996 there were 2,704 companies on the main market (2,171 UK companies and 533 international). The market is highly active, which means it is easy to buy and sell shares. The average daily turnover in UK equities in 1996 was £2·9bn, with over 43,000 transactions each day.

The Stock Exchange has a number of different functions:
○ It raises new capital for companies.
○ It provides various services connected with the market, such as providing information and making sure trading and settlement

(paying for trade dealings) takes place promptly and efficiently.

○ It regulates companies and market dealers.

In 1996, £157·2bn was raised on the London Stock Exchange and 296 companies were admitted to the market for the first time. Listed companies vary in size from those with less than £1m market capitalisation (tiny in stockmarket terms!) to those with over £90bn. They come from many different sectors of industry.

Companies may seek a Stock Exchange listing to raise new capital in order to develop or expand the firm, or to reduce borrowings. They may also want their shares more widely marketed and traded, and may feel that 'going public' on the stockmarket adds to their status and visibility.

WHAT HAPPENS WHEN A FIRM DECIDES TO SEEK A MARKET LISTING

Let's suppose a business run by a family firm has grown after a number of years to a substantial size. It would like to expand overseas, but hasn't got the capital to take on big international competitors. The company decides to seek an official listing on the Stock Exchange, which means incurring considerable expense. It must satisfy the Exchange that it meets a number of stringent criteria: it must give details of its trading history and financial record, management and future prospects. All this goes into a document called the 'listing particulars'. It must also put a minimum percentage of its stock into public hands.

Its owners, who have hitherto controlled the company, must agree to give up a percentage of their ownership to public shareholders, who will have a say in the future running of the company. On the other hand, rather like releasing capital tied up in a house, the owners can now sell their own shareholding on the market if they want to convert it into cash.

The listing application is handled by a sponsoring firm approved by the Exchange. Once the Exchange has accepted its application for listing, a launch date is agreed. Investors can buy shares for the first time, and the company gets the capital it wants.

Raising capital in this way is known as the 'primary market'. Once the money has been raised by the initial sale of shares, the shares can be bought and sold freely in the market as long as there are investors who want to buy and sell. This is called the 'secondary market'. It means that the investor is not locked in to his

London's top 20

The 20 largest UK companies quoted on the Stock Exchange (at 6.8.97)

		Market capitalisation £m
1	HSBC Holdings	59,974
2	British Petroleum	50,967
3	Glaxo Wellcome	47,521
4	Shell	47,040
5	Lloyds TSB	41,326
6	SmithKline Beecham	33,113
7	British Telecommunications	26,580
8	Barclays	20,151
9	Zeneca	19,401
10	Halifax	18,486
11	Marks & Spencer	16,844
12	BAT Industries	15,732
13	Unilever	15,192
14	National Westminster Bank	14,398
15	Cable & Wireless	13,415
16	Grand Metropolitan	12,517
17	Prudential	11,910
18	Abbey National	11,896
19	Reuters	11,629
20	Guinness	11,181

Source: FTSE International Ltd

HOW THE STOCKMARKET WORKS

or her investment, but can sell whenever he or she wants. The company does not make money directly out of share dealing on the secondary market, but it is in the interest of all shareholders for shares to be in demand, so that prices are buoyant or rising.

A company which is listed may want to raise more capital in the future, which will lead to further share issues. It can also raise loan capital. Loan issues are dealt with in detail in Chapter 8.

The main market is known as the Official List. It is designed for substantial companies which can afford its onerous and expensive listing requirements. The table on page 29 lists the top twenty UK companies quoted as at August 1997, including the newly arrived Halifax, which leapt in near the top following the building society's demutualisation in May the same year. Demutualisation means the company launched itself on the stockmarket, ceasing to be owned only by its policyholders.

Apart from UK stocks, companies quoted include international firms from many countries. New companies admitted to the market in 1996 included five from India and three from Korea. India is one of the fastest growing emerging markets represented on the stockmarket. Others are South Africa, Thailand and Malaysia.

For smaller companies which need a simpler way in to the stockmarket, there is the Alternative Investment Market (AIM). Launched in June 1995, AIM is designed for 'small, young and growing companies'. There is no size requirement, no minimum number of shares in public hands, and no need for companies to have a lengthy trading record. At the end of 1996 there were 252 AIM companies, of which 145 were admitted during the year, and 15 AIM market makers.

AIM companies also come from a wide range of sectors. High-tech companies and leisure and restaurant operators are perhaps regarded as typical AIM sectors, though there are older companies and companies from more traditional sectors as well.

Shares in AIM companies are among the most risky the Stock Exchange has to offer. These are young, speculative companies

Independent financial adviser and *Moneywise* Ask the Professionals panellist Brian Dennehy says:

"AIM mostly concentrates on smaller companies with with limited track records. The shares won't be as easy to buy and sell as those with full listing, and research on these companies tends to be limited. But if you know something about a particular AIM company and its marketplace, you could uncover an interesting speculative investment."

trading more on their future prospects than on a list of past successes. They may also be less liquid than companies on the Official List – that is, there may be fewer people who are prepared to buy and sell shares, and correspondingly lower volumes of dealing, so investors may find it hard to sell at an acceptable price.

How it works

BEFORE BIG BANG the stockmarket was similar to any other market in that it had a trading floor and dealers' 'stalls', with brokers who walked around the market buying and selling person-to-person with jobbers. The trading floor fell silent very shortly after the market reforms, and trading is now done by computer.

The Stock Exchange employs a great deal of sophisticated modern technology, notably SEAQ – the Stock Exchange Automated Quotations Service. This is a continually updated database which distributes market makers' bid (buying) and offer (selling) prices. Market makers must, throughout the daily trading period (08.30 to 16.30, Monday to Friday), display bid and offer prices for all the securities in which they are registered to make a market.

Brokers can keep constantly up to date on prices by viewing SEAQ on their screens. They will choose the most competitive price for their needs, and deal with that market maker. This is known as the competing broker system. (For an example of how this actually works, see Chapter 9.)

The 'yellow strip' on the SEAQ screen identifies the best bid and offer price from the investor's point of view for every SEAQ security, with up to four market makers who are quoting these prices. SEAQ International offers a similar service for international securities, and SEATS PLUS for less liquid stocks, including AIM stocks.

○ *SETS*, the Stock Exchange Electronic Trading Service, will create a significant change in the way the market works. It should also make dealing faster and cheaper and give access to better information.

SETS will mean that the competing broker system will be abandoned on the market's larger stocks in favour of a system known as order-matching. Prices will be displayed on an electronic order book, but instead of brokers phoning up to trade at the most competitive price, buyers and sellers will automatically be matched on screen. Orders will remain in the computer system until a deal is executed, or the order is deleted, or a specified expiry time is reached.

SETS will operate initially on FTSE 100 stocks only. The service is not expected to expand to more than the top 300 stocks, as order-matching systems are most efficient where stocks are very liquid (that is, very frequently traded). As far as the private investor is concerned, SETS should lead to smaller spreads (the difference between the bid and offer price) and therefore better prices.

○ CREST is the electronic system which 'settles' trades, making sure stock is delivered and paid for. The way it works and its implications for private investors are discussed in Chapter 9.

DIFFERENT TYPES OF SHARE

Ordinary shares: If you hold shares in a company, they will probably be ordinary shares. Each ordinary share represents an equal proportion of the company's share capital. If a company has a million shares, someone who holds 1,000 shares owns 0·1% of the company and has pro rata voting rights.

Ordinary shareholders have the following benefits:

○ Dividends, which are a share of the company's earnings, and perhaps the most attractive and valuable shareholder benefit.

○ Access to the annual report and accounts and other information of importance about the company.

○ Future shares issues like rights issues or scrip issues (see Chapter 4).

○ The right to attend the company's annual general meeting (AGM), which must be called once a year. Shareholders must be given notice of the date and time meeting, at which they are entitled to speak.

○ The right to vote on issues affecting the company. This includes the appointment and dismissal of directors and auditors, and any event which might dilute existing shareholdings – such as an issue of more shares in the company (like a rights issue) or an employee share scheme. It might also include a decision on whether or not to accept a takeover bid.

○ Limited rights to initiate change. Shareholders with at least 5% of the company's capital between them can put forward a motion at the AGM. A group of shareholders representing at least 10% of total capital can force the board to call an extraordinary general meeting (EGM). The latter in particular is very rare, given the difficulty of getting together so many investors.
○ The so-called 'shareholder perks' available to shareholders in some companies. These are fringe benefits, usually related to the business of the company concerned. Typically they might be discount vouchers or tokens giving free goods and services. They tend to be popular with shareholders. They are discussed at greater length in Chapter 4.

The traditional proof that you own the shares is a share certificate, which gives the name of the company and the number of shares you own. You will get it from the company's registrars, who maintain the shareholder register, some time after dealing. On the back of the certificate is a transfer form which you fill in when you want to sell shares.

Nowadays the market is moving more towards 'paperless dealing', where share certificates are done away with in favour of a computer record held by a nominee company. However, many private investors still prefer to hold on to their certificates.

Occasionally companies have shares in issue which have reduced, or no, voting rights. Usually designed to help keep control of the company in the hands of a small group of shareholders, shares like this are discouraged by the Stock Exchange and are not often available. The 'golden share' which the government retained in some of the privatisation issues had super-voting rights. It could be used to veto decisions by the company which might have major national significance.

Partly paid shares: New issues of shares are sometimes 'partly paid'. This is as it sounds – you pay only part of the price at the outset, and the balance of the money is due at fixed dates in the future. The price will go down as the payment date comes up, and will bounce up again once the shares are 'fully paid'.

Preference shares: These are a type of ordinary share whose shareholders get a 'preferred' dividend. This means that the dividend has to be paid before dividends to ordinary shareholders can be distributed, and preference shareholders rank ahead of ordinary shareholders if the company goes into liquidation. Preference dividends are normally fixed, and, as a result, they tend to be bracketed with fixed-interest investments. They are dealt with in more detail in Chapter 5.

Q&A

Q The word 'equities' is used a lot in writing about investment. What does it mean?

A 'Equities' is used to mean shares in companies, as opposed to fixed-interest investments or cash deposits. It echoes the fact that each ordinary share represents an equal share of the ownership of the company.

Q I was recently given some windfall shares by a demutualising building society. They were described as '25p ordinary shares' on the share certificate, but on the first day they were worth over £3 each. Can you explain?

A Ordinary shares have a face value, or par value, when they are first issued, which may be 25p each, or 10p or £1. As you have found out, the par value may bear no relation at all to the actual value of the shares on the stockmarket. You can ignore the face value, which is a historical anomaly, though to identify the shares for some formal purposes you will need to quote their full title, for instance 'XYZ PLC 25p ordinary shares'.

Q Is it true that you cannot get reports and accounts of companies whose shares you own, if you hold the shares through nominees?

A Yes. If you want to get reports and accounts you may have to avoid holding through nominees, which is a form of safe-keeping which removes the need for you to hold certificates. See what the options are in Chapter 9.

Q I bought some shares in a partly paid issue. Can I sell them again before I have paid for them in full?

A Yes, you are allowed to buy and sell partly paid shares. They will be shown in the press with 'pp' next to the price.

The return on your investment

HAVING RISKED HIS or her assets by investing in shares, what can the private investor hope for in return?

Over the years, dividends will contribute a large part of the total wealth generated by a shareholding. The 1997 BZW Equity-Gilt Study concluded: 'Dividends account for around two thirds of total returns to equities over long periods of time'. Though the amount is not fixed and can go up and down like the share price, dividends are the 'income' from a share investment. The dividend is quoted as 'yield' (or the dividend per share represented as a percentage of the current share price).

Ordinary shareholders are normally paid dividends twice a year. The mid-year payment is called the 'interim' dividend. It coincides with the interim report on the company's progress. Dividends are decided on by the board of directors, which pays them out of the company's after-tax earnings. The amount paid will reflect how well the company has been doing and is likely to do in the near future.

If conditions are good, dividends are set at a level to equal or improve on the amount paid last year. If the company is going through hard times, dividends may be reduced or even cancelled altogether. Equity dividends at times of high interest rates cannot compete with the rates of interest offered by building societies and banks. When interest rates are low – as they have been for a number of years – the income from shares looks much more attractive. For long-term investors, shares offer the chance of dividend growth as well as share price growth – a much better prospect than that from gilts or deposits.

Dividends will vary from company to company, with some offering a high yield, and others little or nothing in the way of dividends. A start-up technology company which is going through an initial research and development stage may have a delay before producing significant earnings. Such a company is unlikely to pay dividends at the outset. On the other hand some sectors are traditionally high yielders. Some major companies have a long record of dividend payment which has remained stable or has increased. For such a company it would be a big setback to have to reduce a dividend payout.

If you take an interest in the stockmarket you will soon come across the terms 'ex dividend' (xd) and 'cum dividend' (cd). These terms are related to the cut-off date whereby the market decides who is entitled to receive a forthcoming dividend.

For example, a company announces that it will pay a dividend on a certain date. At a fixed date before that pay date the stock will go ex-dividend. After that date anyone who buys the stock will not get the dividend – instead it will go to the seller. The xd date is merely a technicality, reflecting the fact that the share register cannot be instantly adjusted to reflect ownership. However, it does affect prices: when the stock goes ex-dividend its price will also go down, roughly reflecting the value of the payout. Share price listings given in the newspapers will show whether or not the stock is xd.

When the stock is not xd it is cd, or cum dividend, though this is not normally shown in price listings, as it is more important to be aware of the xd trading period. If there is no mention of xd you can assume the stock is trading cum dividend.

WHY SHARE PRICES MOVE

The other type of return which the investor is looking for is capital growth, through an increase in the price of shares. Though dividends can rise and fall, or even be missed out altogether, changes in the share price are even less predictable.

The mechanism which drives share prices is supply and demand – if there are more buyers than sellers the price has to go up to persuade more holders to part with shares. If there are more investors wanting to offload shares than there are to buy, prices will have to fall to persuade buyers that they are getting a good deal.

But what makes people want to buy or sell? Here are a number of the main reasons why share prices move.

Independent financial adviser and *Moneywise* Ask the Professionals panellist Brian Dennehy says:

"Share prices move because there are more buyers than sellers. You can try and explore why buyers are buying, but the motivations will vary enormously – early buyers may be motivated by a company's profit potential, later ones will simply be mimicking early buyers. Most people should buy quality shares and hold them for the long term."

○ *Bad news or good news?* Good or bad news affecting a company's business will affect the share price.
Good: A leisure shoes company sees a boom in demand for its product after a pop group which has rocketed to the top of the charts is seen wearing them.
Bad: A company which produces a household name brand of tinned meat sees its price plummet following widespread publicity after an insect is found in a tin.

○ *Finding favour*: The industrial sector in which a company finds itself is in favour or out of favour.
In favour: As the Internet gives a new boost to the world-wide enthusiasm for home computing, all companies involved in the industry will benefit from the craze. The boost to their share prices also rubs off onto retailers, distributors' hardware manufacturers and other types of company that are associated with the market.
Out of favour: During a big slump in the housing market construction companies and property developers see hard times, and share prices are dragged down. The fall in values extends to all types of company which manufacture and sell electrical goods, furniture, kitchens, double glazing and other related consumer durables – all of which are closely related to the housing market.

○ *Market moves*: The market as a whole rises or falls. However good the fortunes of an individual company, it will to an extent follow the market. If the stockmarket experiences a boom, the effect will be felt everywhere. In the same way a big fall in share prices (sometimes known euphemistically as a 'market correction') will take everything with it – from the giant conglomerate down to the smallest stocks quoted.

○ *Economic factors*: Changing economic factors affect the stockmarket in general and may also affect particular sectors. Rising inflation and interest rates are bad for business in general, but some types of company may be particularly sensitive. A financial company whose business is making loans, and a company selling sofas which are usually bought on credit, will both suffer if interest rates rise. Retailers whose business does not depend so much on credit will be less affected. If the pound is strong against other currencies, exporting companies will be badly hit.

○ *Mergers and acquisitions*: Because a quoted company is publicly owned, it is possible for another company to build up a shareholding and take over ownership. Likewise, two companies which feel their business aims are similar and that they would benefit from greater mass might merge. Takeovers and mergers can be good or bad as far as the market is concerned:
Good: A large holding company, whose business consists of acquiring other concerns and honing them to maximum profitability, is thought to be interested in a medium-sized car hire company based in the Midlands. The holding company has had a long record of strong performance in a wide range of industries. Once the rumour breaks, the car hire company's shares rise sharply.
Bad: A large company has been performing indifferently for some time. In an attempt to bring it round, a new chief executive is brought in and restructuring begins. Part of the strategy is to rationalise the areas of business in which the company is involved. Several subsidiaries which do not fit in are disposed of, and to strengthen its food manufacturing arm the company wants to acquire a successful manufacturer of snack products. The feeling in the market is not favourable: is the large company overstretching itself, when it would be wiser to retrench? Its share price drops when the acquisition is announced.

○ *Great expectations:* The future prospects of a company, according to the expectations of the market, can make a difference to the share price.
Good: A medium-sized regional business has been supplying fast food outlets for years. Recently, it has come up with a new product which it intends to market directly through its own outlets. Investors feel that the company is well run, marketing is good, and the company's estimate of the demand for the new product is realistic. Many are persuaded to buy into its promising future, and this is reflected in the share price.
Bad: A large company in the process of restructuring (see above) has had little success. Its disposals have not raised the

amount of cash expected, and it has made an ill-timed acquisition which has turned into a drain on resources. City analysts predict that its next annual report will show a significant fall in profits. The share price suffers accordingly.

This is just a selection of the main factors affecting share prices. Sometimes it is hard to pinpoint why prices rise and fall. 'Market sentiment' – or the consensus among investors regarding a company's fortunes – may be the reason given for fluctuating share prices.

Large firms of stockbrokers will have teams of researchers whose job is to follow the fortunes of companies and make recommendations on whether to buy or sell the stock. If you are a frequent investor, or deal regularly with a stockbroker, you can tap into this sort of information. If you are keen on running your own portfolio, or you belong to an investment club, you may want to do some research of your own, through any source available, but mainly through the media.

Some of the excitement of investment lies in spotting something about a company which may cause its shares to go up in price, and which has not been noticed by other investors. This is unlikely to happen with the largest companies because they are heavily researched by major brokers and there is very little news about them which is not already taken account of in the share price.

Smaller companies are different: they are not so well-researched, and you are much more likely to find out something that could have a future affect on share prices. You may even have local knowledge of a company which puts you one step ahead of the big London broker.

There is a caveat here: if you work for the company and are aware of confidential information which could affect the share price, you cannot use that knowledge to buy or sell shares. This is called 'insider dealing' and it is illegal.

INDICES

Individual shares may move up or down from day to day, but the market overall also has its own momentum. This is measured by averaging the movement of individual companies to produce market indices.

The main market indices

Index	Approx. mkt. cap. of constituents	% size	Calculation frequency
FTSE 100	Above £1.8bn	75.5	real time
FTSE Mid 250	£280m–£1.8bn	18.0	real time
FTSE Actuaries 350	liquid benchmark	93.5	real time
FTSE Small Cap	£40m–£280m	4.5	real time
FTSE Actuaries All-Share	Above £40m	98.0	end of day
FTSE Actuaries Fledgling	Below £40m	1.5	end of day

Source: London Stock Exchange

The index gives a broad guide as to how the market is performing and serves as a measure. Managers of investment funds and pensions, for instance, will compare the performance of their chosen portfolios to the index to see whether they have done better or worse than the market average.

All world markets have their own index. Large markets will have more than one index, usually divided between larger and smaller companies, though individual sectors may also have their own index.

In London there is a full range of indices: the two main series are the FTSE indices and the FT/S&P Actuaries World indices. The initials derive from the *Financial Times* newspaper, the Stock Exchange and the Institute and Faculty of Actuaries – the three bodies which have worked to develop the indices that are in use today.

The table above lists the main indices used. Perhaps the most famous is the FTSE 100 – the Footsie – which consists of the 100 largest UK companies. Also well known is the FTSE A All-Share, a major benchmark for fund performance, which covers quoted companies with capitalizations of more than £40m. As the table above shows, this includes almost the whole market.

The FTSE 250 index includes the 250 next largest companies after the FTSE 100. The FTSE 350 combines the companies in these two indices and, based on its constituents, sector indices are calculated, known as industry baskets. The FTSE Small Cap measures the performance of about 550 smaller companies and the FTSE Fledgling includes all companies too small to be included in the All-Share Index.

Some indices are recalculated every minute to give a 'real time' impression of what is happening in the market. Others are only calculated once a day, at the end of trading.

Indices are used in derivatives markets, where 'futures' and 'options' – forms of betting on future market movements, based on index performance – can be traded by investors. Indices also form the basis for 'passive investment', where a fund manager aims to reproduce the performance of the market as a whole by shadowing the movements of the index. This approach, known as tracking, is dealt with further in Chapter 5.

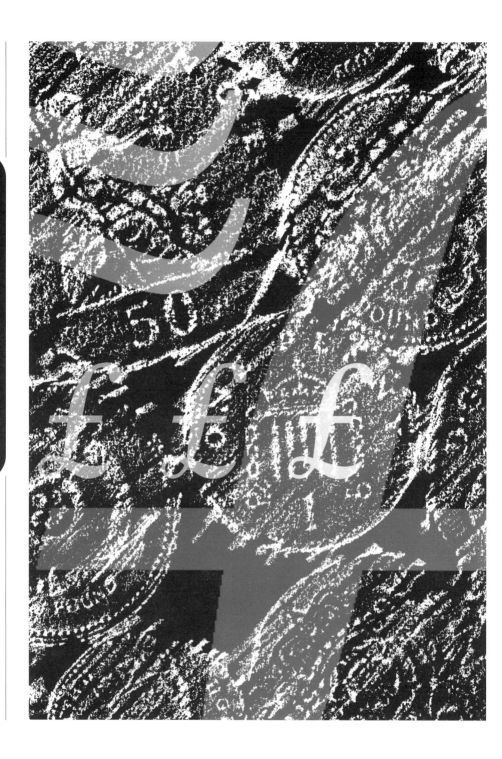

3 Deciding which shares to buy

One of the keys to investing in the stockmarket is information. This chapter explains how to interpret and make the most of the different sources of information about companies quoted on the Stock Exchange.

Stock assessment

IF YOU HAVE no experience of share investment the 'report and accounts' will be a daunting document. If you are serious about learning more, you will have to study its contents and translate what is often seemingly impenetrable jargon into more meaningful terms.

The report and accounts: Quoted companies are obliged to disclose a good deal of information about themselves. They do so every year in their 'report and accounts' which is sent out to shareholders. Half way through the year there will also be an interim report, showing the year's progress to date.

Points to remember
- Some companies, especially large companies conscious of good investor relations, are doing their best to make company reports more user-friendly. But there are still plenty of examples of reports filled with unfamiliar jargon.
- There is a limit to what can be learnt solely from the accounts. Find out more about the company from the press and other sources.
- Nobody likes to give away more about themselves than they have to – and companies are no exception. Whilst companies will fulfil their legal disclosure obligations, they won't go out of their way to highlight a problem.
- Big business is complex and it may not always be easy to pick out what is happening in the company just from the accounts.

○ It is hard to lay down accounting rules which result in completely standard presentation of company information – one company may record a certain aspect of its business differently from a competitor. This makes it hard for the investor to compare the two.

○ Figures shown in brackets in the accounts are negative amounts.

○ You can make most sense of the accounts by comparing them to previous years' figures.

○ The accounts are a snapshot of what was happening in the company at a certain date, usually some months before the report reaches your hands. Remember this when reading them.

THE MAIN SECTIONS ARE:

○ *The financial summary*: Selected highlights of performance, sometimes giving a number of years of historical comparison. See page 46 for an annotated summary.

○ *Chairman's report:* A carefully worded PR document which may not be all that informative. Some reading between the lines may be necessary.

○ *Directors' report:* More information on the company's activities during the year. Changes to the board and political and charitable donations will be included.

○ *Auditors' report:* If the accounts are not properly presented in some way the auditors will indicate they are not happy with them. However, this is a very rare occurrence. It is far more likely that any problems will have been settled to the auditors' satisfaction before the report is printed.

○ *Balance sheet:* Statement of the company's assets and liabilities – the property it owns and anything it owes. Fixed assets are things like buildings or machinery. Current assets include cash, money owed to the company, stock and raw materials. Liabilities include any amount owing to creditors, overdrafts, payments due on loans, tax and national insurance. Current liabilities are payable within a year.

Companies which have subsidiaries produce group accounts, with a consolidated balance sheet which shows the assets and liabilities of all the businesses combined.

○ *Profit and loss account:* This shows the extent to which the company's income from sales has exceeded its costs. If the costs are higher, the company has made a loss! Turnover is the amount of sales made in the year. The profit for the year after tax, and after the deduction of minority shareholders' interests (other owners of partly owned subsidiaries) is what is left for distribution to shareholders. It is sometimes called 'attributable profits'. The accounts will break it down into the amount the company has earned per share ('earnings per share') and the amount the directors have decided to pay as dividends ('dividend per share'). The difference between the two is put back into the business.

O *Cash flow:* This shows the company's cash position – cash raised from activities like a new share issue or the sale of an asset, and spent on things like repaying loans or acquiring new assets. Cash is important in a company – if there is not enough of it, the company will go bust.

O *Notes to the accounts:* The notes may appear to be the most impenetrable part of the report and accounts, but they can contain important nuggets of information – for instance, directors' pay, share options and shareholdings; changes in their shareholdings (whether they have bought or sold shares); the major shareholders; further details of sales and profits; and any unusual items.

READING THE ACCOUNTS

Points to watch out for:

O *Turnover:* If turnover is up, profits and earnings per share should also grow. Turnover is a key indicator.

O *Cash flow* is another important sign of whether the company is healthy. If cash balances are falling, the company could ultimately become insolvent.

O *Pre-tax profits* should show a rising trend along with turnover if the business is doing well. Don't rely on profit figures alone – there are accounting methods, often referred to as 'massaging', which can be used to make them seem larger.

O *Interest charges:* What is the trend here? If charges are up, is it due to increased borrowings or higher interest rates?

O *Dividends:* Are they up on last year? Comparing them to earnings per share tells you a lot about dividend policy in the company. In the example shown on page 46, dividends rose smoothly though earnings have been more volatile.

Profit & loss account
This section shows how much money the company has made or lost on its turnover. The profit is what is left after costs – payments to suppliers, staff, other overheads and tax. Some profit is paid to shareholders, the rest is ploughed back into the company

Five year financial summary

YEARS ENDED 31 MARCH

1992	1992	1993	1994	1995	1996
1992	£m	£m	£m	£m	£m
Profit and loss account					
Turnover	13,337	13,242	13,675	13,893	14,446
Operating profit (a)	3,370	2,403	2,982	2,663	3,100
Group's share of profits of associated undertakings	7	13	18	92	82
Profit (loss) on sale of group's undertakings	–	(132)	(14)	241	7
Net interest payable	304	256	230	259	170
Premium on repurchase of bonds	–	56	–	75	–
Premium on ordinary activities before taxation	3,073	1,972	2,756	2,662	3,019
Tax on profit on ordinary activities	999	724	951	926	1,027
Profit on ordinary activities after taxation	2,074	1,248	1,805	1,736	1,992
Minority interests	30	28	38	5	6
Profit for the financial year	2,044	1,220	1,767	1,731	1,986
Earnings per shares	33·2p	19·8p	28·5p	27·8p	31·6p
Dividends per share	14·4p	15·6p	16·7p	17·7p	18·7p
Cash flow statement					
Net cash inflow before operating activities	5,710	5,127	4,914	5,113	5,829
Interest paid less returns on investments	(351)	(314)	(184)	(324)	(125)
Dividends paid	(859)	(931)	(1,014)	(1,083)	(1,158)
Net cash outflow from returns on investments and servicing of finance	(1,210)	(1,245)	(1,198)	(1,407)	(1,283)
Tax paid	(897)	(975)	(605)	(1,175)	(784)
Purchase of tangible fixed assets	(2,565)	(2,148)	(2,161)	(2,638)	(2,547)
Purchase of subsidiary undertakings and investments	(52)	(27)	(612)	(2,395)	(233)
Net (purchase) disposal of short-term investments	(416)	327	(463)	1,934	(524)
Other investing activities	95	92	168	238	148
Net cash outflow from investing activities	(2,938)	(1,756)	(3,068)	(2,861)	(3,156)
Net cash inflow (outflow) before financing	665	1,151	43	(330)	606
Balance sheet					
Tangible fixed assets	15,785	15,736	15,584	16,012	16,496
Fixed asset investments	660	735	1,312	1,082	1,057
Net current assets (liabilities)	(150)	322	125	(725)	(106)
Total assets less current liabilities	16,295	16,793	17,021	16,369	17,447
Loans and other borrowing falling due after one year	(3,768)	(3,386)	(3,199)	(3,361)	(3,322)
Provisions for liabilities and charges	(665)	(1,117)	(701)	(879)	(1,267)
Minority interests	(108)	(72)	(95)	(132)	(180)
Total assets less liabilities	11,754	12,218	13,026	11,997	12,678

(a) Operating profit for the years ended 31 March 1992 to 1995 has been restated for a reclassification of the annual charge for the employee share ownership scheme

Check whether the profit is growing and if so, whether earnings per share are up

Cashflow statement
This section shows what cash the company has generated from activities, such as buying and selling assets or issuing new shares, and what it has spent on activities, such as repaying loans

Check whether this figure includes any exceptional items, such as one-off sales of assets. This can distort profits

Balance sheet
This section shows the companies assets and liabilities. Current assets include cash, money in the bank and stock. Fixed assets include buildings and equipment, royalties, patents and copyrights. Liabilities include overdrafts, money owed to suppliers and taxes due in the short and long term

Check a company's borrowing position in relation to its net assets or shareholder funds. Alarm bells should ring if net debt is more than 100% of net assets but borrowing of 50% or more of assets could be a good sign. If borrowings are less than 50% this could mean the company has a cash surplus

○ *Other questions to ask:*
- If costs or taxes are up, find out why.
- Are there any exceptional items which make a difference to the figures?
- Have there been any changes in accounting policies? If so, why?
- Have there been major pay rises for directors? Have directors sold big blocks of shares? Ask yourself why.

RATIOS

Those who study company accounts use a number of ratios to help them compare one company with another. A ratio is a figure based on the relationship of one financial aspect of the business to another. It is important to compare ratios with other companies in the same sector, and with the sector average.

The most common ratios are:

○ *The price-earnings or p/e ratio* (current share price divided by earnings per share – earnings per share is after tax profits divided by the number of shares in issue):

This ratio is widely used as a shorthand guide to how well the market rates a company. A historic p/e uses the current share price and the latest profits. A prospective p/e uses projected future figures. The higher the p/e, the better rated the company – it shows how many times earnings investors are prepared to pay for the shares, or how much they expect earnings to grow. The p/e ratio moves in the opposite direction from the yield.

○ *Dividend cover* (earnings divided by dividends): This shows how comfortably (or otherwise) the company can afford to pay its dividends. The higher the ratio, the more investors can expect increasing dividends in future years. If cover is low, the company may be in danger of cutting a dividend.

○ *Gearing* (net borrowings divided by shareholders' funds and minority interests): This shows how important borrowings are to the company. The lower the gearing ratio, the better. Gearing of 50% of net assets is regarded as OK. Much more than that, and the company could be badly burdened by debt and vulnerable to increases in interest rates.

DECIDING WHICH SHARES TO BUY

○ The *acid test ratio* (current assets excluding stock divided by current liabilities): This measures the company's liquidity – how easy would it be for it to pay short-term creditors? Stock is excluded because the company might not be able to rely on turning it into cash quickly. If the two sides of the calculation are roughly equal – that is, the ratio is around 1 – the position is healthy. If the ratio is less than 1, the company could not meet its short-term liabilities.

○ *Return on capital employed* (profit before tax divided by shareholders' funds): This measures how much the company is making compared to the capital put into the business. If the return on capital is not high enough, the company will have trouble funding its borrowings. A company which is doing well should have a return on capital of at least 20%.

Other figures which you may see mentioned in company commentaries are net asset value and margins. Net asset value (NAV) is shareholders' funds (total assets less total liabilities) divided by the number of shares in issue. If the NAV is higher than the share price, shareholders can be reassured that the assets of the business alone are enough to cover the cost of their investment. On the other hand, this means the company would be worth more to them if it ceased trading and sold all its assets. It could also be attractive to asset-stripping predators. NAVs are particularly relevant to the investment trust sector (see Chapter 6).

There are various ways of calculating margins, which are basically profits as a percentage of sales, and represent a quick guide to company profitability.

Q&A

Q *I receive a short report each year on the progress of my holding in a former building society, now a bank. I understand this is not the full report and accounts. Should I ask to see the fuller version?*

A The regulations allow companies to send

Independent financial adviser and *Moneywise* Ask the Professionals panellist Kean Seager says:

"Remember ratios in themselves are not good or bad. In assessing whether they are giving a 'buy' or 'sell' signal, you need to look at an individual company's ratios and compare them with their own history and with the market average. I always like to look at p/e ratios and net asset value ratios."

out a short summary report instead of the full report and accounts, and a number of companies do so. Many shareholders do not spend much time reading the report and accounts, so they are happy with this. But if you want to follow your company's progress in detail, you need the full version.

Q *I want to choose my own share investments through a self-select PEP, but I gather you can't receive the report and accounts if you invest in this way. Is there any way round this?*

A You are right in thinking that PEP holders do not automatically get reports, whether on individual companies or on investment funds. This is due to the fact that your investment is held through nominees (see Chapter 9). However, a few self-select PEPs will get the reports and accounts for you as part of the service. Others will do it for a charge.

ASSESSING STOCKS

○ Set out to learn the language and implications of annual reports. If you have a stockbroker who is friendly and helpful, ask lots of questions.

○ Get full reports and accounts for stocks you own and analyse them as best you can, working out ratios where appropriate.

○ You can also get annual reports for companies where you are not a shareholder. Ask through the company's head office. The *Financial Times* offers a report ordering service in a number of companies quoted in its prices pages.

○ Compare this year's figures to previous years and consider any observable trends.

○ Ask questions of the company itself if anything is unclear. Large companies have investor relations departments which should be happy to help, although they won't give answers on commercially sensitive issues.

○ Follow your company's progress in the press. Look in the city pages of your newspaper and specialist financial publications. There will be comment in the media when your company's annual report is published, so you can compare notes with the experts.

○ Specialist trade publications may be relevant. For instance, if you are investing in a computer company which brings out a new product, computing magazines will review it and give their opinion. This in turn may give you an impression of how likely the company is to increase sales.

○ Don't forget to compare your company to its sector, which is a good way of getting a perspective on its performance.

○ Attend the annual general meeting. Anyone who holds at least one share can attend and ask questions. You might have to submit any questions in advance.

○ Once you own shares, don't forget to keep an eye on them. Don't allow yourself to get upset by day-to-day ups and downs in the price, but be alert for more serious changes in price trend, or for news which may affect your company's fortunes.

Strategies for choosing

THERE IS A good deal of folklore surrounding the choosing of shares. Recommended strategies range from the ranks of the old wives tale to highly technical systems accessible only to the expert.

Before you start, there are two golden rules:

1 *Have a strategy*
   It may be very simple, and may not amount to much more than a basic philosophy of investment, but a rationale of some sort is better than making unrelated, haphazard choices.

2 *Bear in mind your risk profile*
   Your strategy should not cut across your risk tolerance level. The following section on risk gives some general ideas on how to manage volatility – don't be tempted into a fashionable, small high-tech company if you want low-risk, long-term investments with a high yield.

   Here is a checklist of some of the main investment strategies. Some of them are more appropriate to the fund manager than the private investor, but they do throw some light on how the professionals think when they are making investment choices. First, some strategies the smaller investor can relate to:

○ *Investing in the high street:* The idea of this is to spot companies with which you come into contact day-to-day, and use

Independent financial adviser and *Moneywise* Ask the Professionals panellist Kean Seager says:

"Your own investment strategy depends very much on your investment goals and your risk profile. Once you have established this you can set about choosing which shares – or unit trusts and investment trusts – to buy. Always ensure your money is well spread even if you're the sort of investor who likes to take high risks."

your own basic observations to assess their likely success. Perhaps a new furniture store has recently opened a huge branch near you. You are impressed with its style and prices. Then a friend in another city mentions that a branch has opened there, too. The company looks good. You decide to invest.

Pros and cons: Your know-how of the markets in which you buy goods is as good as anyone else's – and if you are alert to new developments you may well spot winners. But this strategy has its limits: it is subjective, and it only looks at selected aspects of the company's business – going into the store won't tell you anything about the firm's borrowings – and it also limits you to only one or two sectors. If a slump affects all high street businesses, your portfolio could flop.

○ *Investing in small companies:* This is an appealing strategy. You may have personal knowledge of small companies in your area, and small companies are known to do better than larger ones over the long term. What's more, small companies are capable of much faster growth than big, mature conglomerates because they are starting from a smaller base.

Pros and cons: If you do pick a winner, you could do very well. Smaller companies are less fully researched than industry giants, so you may have a chance to spot something the professionals have not yet picked up on. But the risks are high: small companies have a much higher failure rate than big companies, and although a smaller companies index may outperform the main market over a long period, it can also have long periods of underperformance. For most investors it will be better to use a small companies fund than to rely on your own choices.

○ *Special situations:* These are stocks which have some special reason to attract the investor. They may look likely to be taken over. They may recently have had a major management shake-up which could improve their fortunes. They may be developing a new product which looks like a winner. Companies like this which have done badly in the recent past but look likely to improve are called recovery stocks.

Pros and cons: One of the pros here is the element of fun. Betting on a turnaround in a company's fortunes carries a level of excitement, and great satisfaction for the eagle-eyed investor if the choice is successful. But again the problem is risk. You are, in essence, betting that a single factor will make all the difference.

If you have cash with which you can afford to speculate, go ahead. If not, stick to special situations and recovery funds.

○ *Blue chips:* Blue chip stocks are the famous name, large companies with a steady record. Because they are well known it is easy to find out a lot about them, and they are relatively less risky than smaller, more specialist stocks.

Pros and cons: Holding blue chips reduces the risk element in your portfolio and may also offer good yields. But blue chips are unlikely to perform as dramatically as less familiar names.

○ *Investment sayings:* Most of these are more at the old wives tale end of the strategy spectrum, though some are valuable. Perhaps the most famous is: 'Sell in May and go away, buy back on St Leger's Day' (which is in September). The logic behind this is that markets slump over the summer, so the private investor should put his or her portfolio on ice for its own protection. Unfortunately, you can't rely on this one. It may work in some years, and not in others. The private investor will do better, not by jumping in and out of the market, but by holding shares for the long term.

A wiser saying is: 'It is never too early to take a profit'. When your investments are doing well, holding out for that little bit more is often a recipe for disaster. Leaping out of the roller coaster before it reaches the peak and hurtles down the other side could be very good advice.

○ *Top down or bottom up?* We are now in the realms of the professional investor, where decisions may be made by committee and reinforced by the research of a large team of analysts. In this situation, 'top down' means that the larger considerations are looked at first: is this an appropriate market in which to invest? Are economic conditions such that this market or that sector will benefit? Should we avoid companies in this industry altogether and concentrate on a different market sector?

Having made such decisions, the investment committee will give its pronouncements: the portfolio will be 'overweight' in this or that sector, depending on its prospects in the wider economy. This means the investment portfolio will have a higher percentage of stocks than its size as a constituent of the market index might suggest. It may be 'underweight' in other sectors. Having passed the chosen weightings to the analysts, they will then choose individual stocks.

A 'bottom up' approach means that you start with the stocks and simply choose those which seem like the best investments, without first looking at relative prospects for market sectors.

While private investors cannot work like a professional team, an overall impression of what is happening in the economy and in the different market sectors will help inform investment choice, not forgetting that a spread of sectors is important.

❍ *Value or growth?* 'Value' and 'growth' investment are two well known approaches, whose relative merits are debated by professional investors. They are easy to explain. Value investment tries to seek out companies which are undervalued by the market. In other words, the experts have missed an aspect of the company which suggests it is worth more than its current price. Growth investment tries to catch companies with a record of growing sales and earnings which still have some way to go.

Both methods involve some number-crunching, though they are only more technical expressions of commonsense ideas. The private investor can usefully borrow a little of their philosophy.

❍ *Systems:* Both private individuals and some professionals use investing 'systems'. All this means is that they use a strict formula in order to decide which stocks to buy and sell. This may depend on a couple of favourite ratios, or a broader system such as following charts – chartists use the shape of the share graph itself to predict its future movements. Systems have some value, not least because they force the investor to take a purely dispassionate view. Successful investors must learn to cut their losses on occasion, rather than hanging onto a stock because it 'might come right in the end'.

Building your portfolio

WE ALL DEAL WITH RISK EVERY DAY, and we are aware that some risks are worth taking, while others are not. We have to accept the risk that our homes could be broken into in our absence, but we don't let it prevent us from going out of the front door.

If we have to take risks, we can also take some measures to reduce them. We look both ways before crossing the road, or put an

Examples

○ An elderly investor has very little income, and not much spare cash. He has no money set aside for emergencies. He is a non-taxpayer. He hears that tax-free PEPs are a good idea and puts £2,000 into a unit trust growth PEP.

○ A well-off retired businessman has a large number of assets which he is keeping untouched for future needs. He keeps all his money in bank deposit accounts because he doesn't like the idea of the ups and downs of the stockmarket.

○ A young woman starting her career as a trainee manager at a large retail store doesn't have much cash to spare, but wants to build up savings for the future. She does not expect to call on the money for several years, possibly longer, and has a pension through her employment. She decides how much she can afford each month after careful budgeting – £50 – and puts that amount into the investment trust savings plan of a large general investment trust.

○ A wealthy business executive enjoys running his own investments and is pleased with his own success in choosing investments. A friend who also follows the stockmarket brings to his attention a small company quoted on an overseas smaller companies exchange. After looking at the stock the executive decides it is worth a large investment. He has only £10,000 in free cash, but borrows a further £20,000 in order to invest.

With the exception of the young woman in the third example, all these investors are ill-advised. Though the woman in this example is stretching herself in order to invest, she is putting money away for the long term in a relatively low-risk investment spread.

The first example is committing too much to a high-risk investment, with money which he may need in a hurry. The retired businessman has enough assets to tolerate a degree of risk. But by staying wholly in deposits he may not be building up enough growth to beat inflation.

The wealthy executive should know better. His past successes have made him reckless and he is breaking some golden rules by putting too much money into a highly specialised investment and borrowing to do so. If unforeseen difficulties make his investment fail, and the pound strengthens against the dollar, he will be left with an almost worthless investment – and a large debt.

alarm on the car, for example. These points are also relevant to stockmarket investment:

○ There are risks involved, but investors are prepared to accept them in exchange for better gains.
○ For many investors, accepting a level of stockmarket risk is necessary in order to manage their money properly.
○ There are ways of handling risk which minimise its potential effects on your wealth.

You should make sure the investment risks you take are appropriate. Check your own risk tolerance level, and whether stockmarket investment is acceptable for you (see Chapter 1).

TYPES OF RISK

It helps to identify the various risks attached to stockmarket investment.

○ *Inflation risk:* This is the main type of risk investors face. Equity investments are a good way of countering this risk if you invest over the long term (see Chapter 1).
○ *Market risk:* If you invest in shares or funds, and the price falls, that is called market risk. Stockmarket prices go up and down all the time, so market risk is never absent in any investment that is stockmarket-related. The reason we accept market risk is that over the long term, such investments have the best growth record.
○ *Credit risk:* This only affects fixed-interest investments (see Chapter 8).
○ *Foreign exchange risk:* If you invest overseas you will be subject to the ups and downs of the pound compared to the currency of the country concerned. Currencies also have a bearing on shares or funds in overseas markets.

EXAMPLE

You invest in shares from a country where one pound is worth one dollar (£1 = $1). You buy 100 shares in the national telecom company, also worth $1 each (£100 = $100 = 100 shares). Now suppose the value of the pound falls against the dollar. You can now only buy $0·8 for your pound, but in pound terms your shareholding has grown in value: shares now worth $100 divided by 0·8 = £125. If, instead of falling, the pound rises against the dollar – let's say it is now worth $1·20 – the value of your investment will go down: the shares are now worth $100 divided by $1·20 = £83.

All this assumes that the share price has not changed. If the telecom company's price booms, and the pound falls, you get a 'double whammy' return. If the price booms but the pound rises, growth may be cancelled out.

○ *Liquidity risk:* Liquidity means being able to buy and sell easily because there is plenty of stock available. This might not be the case with a small company, whose shares are rarely traded. If you hold such shares and the price falls, you may not be able to sell them and get your money back. You are then stuck with a growing loss. This is what happened to some investors in smaller companies and investment funds in the 1987 stockmarket crash.

REDUCING RISK

You can help stack the odds in your favour by taking steps to reduce your investment risk. Here is a nine-point risk reduction plan:

1 *Spread your assets:* The principle here is simply 'don't put all your eggs in one basket'. Use a mix of investments which will not leave you too vulnerable to any class of risk.

    Investment advisers commonly talk about dividing your money three ways between cash, shares (equities) and bonds (fixed interest). If you hold all three you will have: cash for emergencies and to avoid market risk; bonds for modest but secure returns with little market risk; and shares for high returns but with a matching high market risk. Spreading your capital between the three asset types means you are putting stockmarket risk into proportion from the start.

2 *Spread your investments:* A spread is important with every class of asset. You should avoid investing all in one company, one market or one sector. An obvious way of buying a spread of investments is to use a fund: a unit trust or an investment trust. If you stick to shares, try and keep at least six to ten holdings. Less than this, and your risk level is very high. Much more, and you will find it hard to keep track of all the companies concerned.

3 *Long-term or short-term?* The 'long term' for stockmarket investments should be at least five years, and preferably ten or more. Those investing for less than five years should stick to investment homes with no market risk.

4 *Stay flexible:* Keeping a spread of investments will help give flexibility to your investment planning. A shift in investment allocation if circumstances change – for example, a move away from the stockmarket and towards high fixed-rate deposits if interest rates rise – can reduce risk.

5 *Direct or through funds?* To spread risk, use investment funds instead of buying shares directly. This applies to investors with

up to £50,000 or even £100,000. Funds spread your money among a large number of holdings – at the least a few dozen and as many as one hundred. You would have to be a very big investor to make this spread viable through direct investment.

6 *Regular savings or lump sum?* The fund investor can choose between investing regular amounts through a savings plan and putting away a lump sum – a choice that is not open to the direct share investor. Regular contributions, apart from being a less painful means of building up savings, also have a specific advantage when it comes to risk. This is the statistical quirk known as 'pound cost averaging'. See page 81 for more details.

7 *General or specialist?* Within the wide range of share investments some carry more risk and some less. There will always be more risk in smaller companies, especially if they are new and dependent on a single and untried product, and especially if they are quoted on overseas markets. An example might be a pharmaceuticals company which is trying to develop a new cancer drug. If its research is successful, the price could take off dramatically. If it is not, the company could disappear, leaving the investor with a total loss.

On the other hand a blue chip company like Marks & Spencer or ICI may offer few surprises. Mature, steady companies like this are unlikely to grow dramatically, but they are also unlikely to go bust. They offer a relatively low risk to the share investor.

8 *Stay at home:* You can eliminate currency risk altogether by keeping all your assets in sterling-based investments. After all, you pay your bills in sterling, and it makes sense to have your assets in the same currency as your liabilities.

Generally, smaller investors (with, say, less than £20,000 to invest) are best advised to avoid the risks that come with foreign exposure. However, a low-risk means of making a small overseas investment is to choose one of the big, well-established, international investment trusts like Foreign & Colonial. Larger investors should hold a spread which includes some international investment.

9 *Product choice:* Some investment funds are specially designed to reduce your overall risk. See Chapter 5 on index tracker and guaranteed funds.

SOME SAMPLE PORTFOLIOS

A rule of thumb for portfolio building is to have a 'core' of lower-risk stocks, plus a small percentage of more exciting satellite holdings. Investors should also keep an eye on costs: frequent dealing, or dealing in foreign or specialist stocks, will push up dealing costs and damage the portfolio's performance.

1 *The low-risk, small investor:* For a very small investor wanting to build a portfolio, funds are the safest bet. A selection of general unit trusts and investment trusts with a strong performance record could be backed by some gilts (to be held to redemption, see Chapter 8) and with some money left in cash for emergency access.

2 *The moderate-risk investor:* This investor can take on board a little risk. With under £50,000, funds only should be used. With investments over that figure brokers may recommend some blue chip holdings. A good spread of investments should be chosen, based primarily on blue chip UK stocks with good dividend records, funds with an international spread, and some gilts, though in a smaller percentage than for the low-risk investor.

3 *The high-risk investor:* An investor with a portfolio which can accept a high level of risk is probably someone wishing to speculate on more 'exciting' specialist investments. This could include some directly held shares in foreign companies (depending on predicted exchange rate movements); some UK smaller companies or special situations; funds investing in emerging markets; and geared investments such as warrants.

4 *The overseas portfolio;* This is for someone who already has a full portfolio of UK stocks and is seeking to diversify overseas. A core holding of international funds could be joined by some blue chip overseas companies, held directly. Unless the size of the portfolio is very large, funds will be more appropriate for foreign fixed-interest, and unavoidable for emerging markets.

5 *The income portfolio:* The exact nature of the portfolio will depend on the amount of income needed, how long it is needed for, and how much growth should be built in. High-income, low risk investors may be better advised to stick to investments with fixed-interest (see Chapter 8). Those needing less income, and with a longer time frame, should pick stocks which have a record of relatively low yields but good growth of dividends.

MISSING OUT ON THE BEST RETURNS

Average annualised investment returns if you were out of the market for the best 10, 20 etc trading days each year (1981-1995)

	In the market continually	MINUS:			
		10 best	20 best	30 best	40 best
	%	%	%	%	%
FTSE A All-Share	18.76	15.47	13.41	11.65	10.04

Source: Fidelity

Held long-term, such stocks will produce good growth of both income and capital. Remember that yield and capital growth are to a degree mutually exclusive: a company paying out high dividends will have less money to plough back into the business, resulting in less growth.

Independent financial adviser and *Moneywise* Ask the Professionals panellist Kean Seager says:

"In truth, the times when you should have bailed out of the stockmarket have been few and far between. Over the years the stockmarket has risen and the investors who have stayed put have done very well. It is extremely difficult to spot the top of a bull market and in general I would say people should stay put unless they have a compelling use for the money in the short to medium term."

When to buy and sell

HOW DO YOU KNOW when to get out of the stockmarket and when to get back in? If you are an expert investor you may have a system which triggers a dealing decision. If not, your best bet is to make a good choice of investments for the long term and then hold on, even if markets fall.

Research has shown that if you sell stocks and are out of the market for only one or two of the best trading days each year, your growth prospects will be badly damaged. Since your chances of choosing to sell and buy back again at exactly the right time are remote, it pays to stay put – though whether you can do so will depend on whether you have access to other funds should an emergency arise while markets are down.

Investment clubs

Finally, if you are interested in learning more about investment but are reluctant to start on your own, an investment club may be the answer.

Investment clubs started as an American phenomenon, but are now gaining popularity in the UK. They allow people to make their own investment choices with the company and support of friends, and without a major financial risk. Many clubs enjoy the social side of their activities as much as the financial side.

Clubs are usually set up by groups of friends, neighbours or work colleagues – it is quite important that the group has an atmosphere of mutual trust. There are all-male and all-female clubs. One of the most famous is the US Beardstown Ladies club, with an average age of 64. Over the club's first ten years the US market grew by 10% a year. The members achieved average growth of over 23%.

EXAMPLE
A group of friends in the same street share an interest in the stockmarket, fuelled by the privatisation shares which some of them hold. One of them reads about investment clubs. They decided to start a club. Each puts in £200 to start, and follows up with £30 a month. They meet once a month to work out strategy, each taking charge of researching or monitoring a few stocks. They soon have a portfolio of several thousand pounds, and their successes more than make up for their failures.

Clubs should be properly constituted and set up, and it is obviously important to get the paperwork right. The club will need a bank account, and may eventually need professional help from stockbrokers and auditors. Some stockbrokers welcome club business, and may even provide speakers for meetings. Valuation, accounts and tax are all important, so someone who is efficient and with a clear head for figures is essential among the membership.

Proshare, the share ownership organisation, can offer detailed help and subsequent support to those interested in setting up clubs.

To get an investment club on the road, you need to be well-organised:

○ *Club structure and officers:* The club should have its own constitution and rules. Officers should include a chairperson, treasurer and secretary, and meetings should have a proper agenda and minutes.

○ *Collecting and holding contributions:* The simplest way to do this is for each member to make a standing order to the club's bank account.

○ *Dealing:* Most purchases and sales of shares will have to be made through a stockbroker (see Chapter 9).

○ *Making investment decisions:* The idea of investment clubs is to share the decision-making democratically, so you need to work out an investment policy that is suitable for all members. In some clubs individual members specialise in different market sectors.

○ *Valuation and accounts:* There is more than one way to value the club's investments. Proshare recommends a 'unit' system.

○ *Tax*: Investment clubs must notify the Inland Revenue when launched and submit a form giving details of income and gains for each club financial year. You're liable to income tax and capital gains tax in the normal way (see Chapter 10).

Action plan

○ Familiarise yourself with company report and accounts – follow the checklist on page 45.

○ Even if you're not keen on maths, get to grips with how different ratios are worked out and how to use this information.

○ Before you start buying and selling work out what your investment strategy is – this will help you make decisions.

○ Always keep in mind the balance in your portfolio and the risks you are taking.

○ If you're keen to start buying shares but aren't keen to go it alone, find out if you can join or set up an investment club.

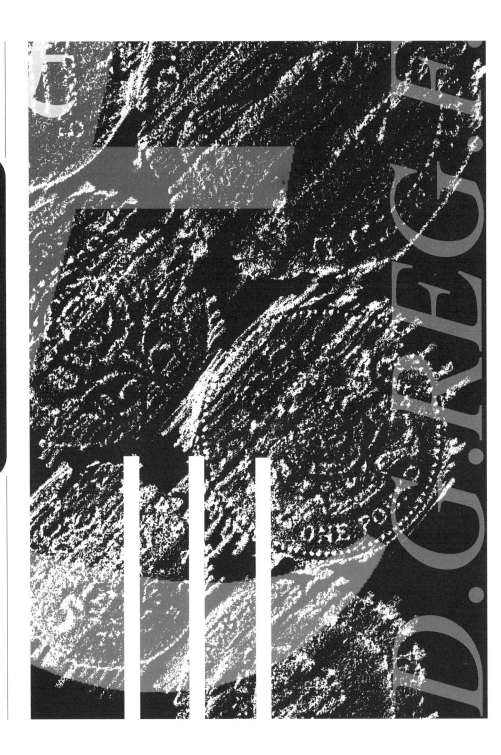

4
Being a shareholder

During the 1980s, largely as a result of the government's privatisation programme, the number of individual shareholders rose from about three million to a peak of eleven million in 1991. In 1993 shareholders represented 22% of the adult population.

In the late 1990s, windfall shares from demutualising building societies and insurers have again given a boost to private share ownership. Windfall shareholders have not had to think about applying for shares, or buying them through a stockbroker. They simply filled in a form and waited for their share certificates to arrive through the post.

New issues

OFFERS FOR SALE

This approach is mostly used in the privatisation issues. Application forms and prospectuses are advertised in the national press and both individuals and institutions can apply for shares. A fixed number of shares is offered at a specified price.

If investors like the offer and think the price is right the issue may be oversubscribed. If this happens, you may not get all the shares you applied for – this is known as 'scaling down'.

The price set in an offer for sale is often conservatively pitched, as the company does not want to see the issue undersubscribed. Shares bought in this way may often, therefore, jump quite a lot in price in the first few days of trading. The razzamatazz and media glitz of privatisation in the 1980s helped bring in investors in enormous numbers, and many saw their shares leaping in value as soon as trading opened.

While this attracted a lot of attention to the stockmarket, it perhaps gave the idea that all new issues will rocket away in price, making a tidy profit for the investor overnight. This is not always the case: if you are thinking of buying shares in an offer for sale, consider all the relevant circumstances first.

A variant on the offer for sale is the 'tender offer'. A minimum price is set and investors are invited to tender for the shares at what they think is an appropriate amount. Once all the applications have been received the advisers to the issue look at the tenders and arrive at a 'strike' price which will be acceptable to the company as well as to the majority of applicants. Tender offers are not as simple to deal with as straightforward offers for sale, so they are not as widely used in issues which are expected to appeal to a wide audience.

Investors who buy shares just for the profit from the initial burst of activity are called 'stags'. Stags will probably sell their shares again in the first day or so of trading. A tender offer greatly reduces the possibility of an issue being 'stagged'.

The stockmarket is traditionally the home of the institutional investor – principally pension funds and insurance companies – and market practice tends to reflect this bias, making life harder for the private investor.

Offers for sale direct to the public only happen nowadays for a few large issues of shares. By and large, new issues are the preserve of the institutions. If you like the idea of buying into new share issues, you must develop a good relationship with a stockbroker who offers a new issue service for private clients. A number of brokers will make arrangements to buy an allocation of shares in a new issue for the use of their clients. A guide to these services is available from ProShare (see Directory).

Independent financial adviser and *Moneywise* Ask the Professionals panellist Kean Seager says:

"New issues can prove very successful, but there have been new issues which have not performed well. The days of big government privatisations are now over and the likelihood of picking up new issues in the bargain basement is going to be very small. They need to be assessed carefully before making an investment."

Inevitably, an investor who deals regularly with a broker will stand more chance of participating in new issue arrangements. Anyone offered shares in this way by a broker should not stag the issue – short-term speculation of this sort is not welcome in a new issue service and may mean you are not offered new issue shares again.

WARRANTS

You may receive some free 'warrants' with your newly issued shares. These are sometimes given by the company as a bonus with new issues, particularly with investment trusts.

Warrants are contracts which give you the right to buy shares at a specified price and on specified dates some time in the future. The share price at which the warrants can be converted (the 'exercise price') will be set some way higher than the issue price. Warrant holders cannot vote and do not receive dividends. If the warrant is not exercised at the appropriate date, then it will expire without value. Warrants can be bought and sold in the market just like shares. They have no value unless they are exercised, and there will be no point in exercising them unless the ordinary share price rises above the warrant exercise price.

If the exercise price is higher than the current share price, warrants are said to be 'out of the money'. If the share price is higher than the exercise price they are 'in the money', and have an inherent value equal to the difference between the two prices.

If you think the share price is likely to rise, warrants represent a cheap way to hold shares, though with a relatively high level of risk: warrant holders are simply betting on a share price at a particular date. However, if your investment is well-judged you could get a geared return – that is, your gain from the warrants will be much higher than the corresponding gain in the share price.

Warrant prices usually rise very fast after issue to stand above (or 'at a premium' to) the share price. Price movements will reflect the fortunes of the ordinary shares, though warrants are a lot more volatile. Premiums vary a lot, but in a rising market they will get smaller as the warrant's life runs out. Buying warrants, though it may not be expensive, is a question of correctly judging the price relationship between the warrant and the ordinary shares.

Some warrant prices are listed with ordinary share price listings in the press, but for more detailed information you will need to consult a stockbroker. See also Chapter 6 for more information on investment trust warrants.

EXAMPLE

You buy some warrants on the shares of a company you like the look of. You pay 91p for each warrant, which gives you the right to subscribe for shares at 177p. The shares currently stand at 240p, so the warrants are 'in the money'. Before the exercise date the share price doubles to 480p. You exercise the warrants. You now hold shares worth 480p. Your profit is 212p (480p less the 177p exercise price and the 91p premium), or 133 % increase on your 91p outlay – though the share price has only risen by 100 %.

Stockmarket events

TAKEOVERS

As a shareholder, technically speaking you have a say in whether or not the company you hold shares in should accept a takeover bid: you will be asked whether you want to sell your shares at the bid price suggested.

In practice, the issue is generally decided not by the private shareholders, but by the big institutional investors who hold significant percentages of the company's shares. So though you may have strong feelings about what is best for the company, the outcome will probably be a fait accompli from your point of view.

The target company may welcome being taken over. Perhaps the potential new parent will solve a problem by bringing stronger financial backing, greater expertise, or an entrée to markets which have proved hard to crack. If so, your company's board will recommend that shareholders accept the offer.

Independent financial adviser and *Moneywise* Ask the Professionals panellist Kean Seager says:

"Takeovers can prove very beneficial to shareholders. Investing with the sole aim of picking takeovers is an extremely tricky business. It's more sensible to pick stocks for their investment potential. If they then become a takeover target, investors may do very well."

If the bid is contested by the target company's board, there could be a drawn-out struggle between predator and target. Each will produce a number of documents, giving detailed arguments, in an attempt to win shareholders' support.

RIGHTS ISSUES

In time, companies may wish to raise further capital. This will result in a rights issue, where existing investors have the right to subscribe for a new issue of shares at a discount to the current price. Rights issues will usually be underwritten by City investing institutions – the institutions agree to take any shares shareholders don't want.

When a rights issue is made the company's share price will drop slightly, to take account of the discount built in to the offer. For example, if you hold shares at £1 and you are offered one more at 85p for every two you hold, the share price should fall to 95p (two

Takeovers: points to consider

1 A COMPANY WHOSE SHARES YOU OWN IS BID FOR. IN THIS SITUATION THERE ARE A NUMBER OF POSSIBLE OUTCOMES:

○ The bid is recommended by the board and goes through without a hitch.

○ The bid is contested, which means the process is lengthy, but is eventually successful.

○ The bid is contested and other companies get involved by mounting a rival bid.

○ The bid is contested and fails.

2 FOR THE SHAREHOLDER, THERE ARE A NUMBER OF POSSIBLE OUTCOMES:

○ You agree to the bid. It is successful. You receive whatever payment has been agreed for your shares.

○ You do not accept the offer (if you don't respond by the date laid down, you are assumed not to have accepted). Further possibilities emerge:
 • Most investors think the same way as you and the offer is rejected. The share price could fall as a result.
 • You are left as part of a small minority of private shareholders. Your shares are hard to deal in because most are tied up in the hands of the predator.
 • You hang on to your shares but you are in such a small minority that the predator is obliged to buy you out, on the same terms as the successful offer. If you ignore this offer, you could be stuck with unsaleable shares – or your shares may be acquired compulsorily.

○ You decide to play it cool and wait, as published figures on acceptances do not come up to the bidding company's hopes. A second bidder comes in with a

better offer than the first. You now have further choices:
 • You can accept the revised bid.
 • You can wait till the last possible minute before deciding whether to accept. In the meantime the share price rises. You now have another option:
 • Sell the shares at a profit and get out.

3 THE PAYMENT OFFERED FOR YOUR SHARES MAY BE IN THE FORM OF:

○ Cash
○ Shares in the bidding company
○ Loan stock issued by the bidding company
○ A combination of any of the three

4 THERE ARE INVESTMENT CONSIDERATIONS ATTACHED TO TAKEOVERS, ON WHICH YOUR STOCKBROKER WILL BE ABLE TO ADVISE. THERE ARE ALSO A NUMBER OF QUESTIONS YOU SHOULD ASK:

○ Do I rate the company a better investment as a subsidiary of the bidder?

○ Is the form of the offer acceptable to my circumstances?

○ What would be the tax consequences for me of accepting the offer? (See Chapter 10.)

○ Is the offer likely to go through with little fuss, or will it be a complicated affair?

○ If a battle is about to ensue, could I make more money by holding out for a better offer, or a rising share price?

○ How committed am I to this company as an investment? If the answer is 'not much', when is the right moment to sell?

shares at £1 each plus one at 85p = £2·85, divided by three shares = 95p). As with dividends, you can buy and sell shares 'ex' or 'cum' rights (see page 36).

As a shareholder you may be offered one new share for, say, every two shares you already own. It is up to you to decide whether or not to take up the issue. Ask yourself some questions about the issue, but take advice from a stock-broker if you are in any doubt.

'Rights' or wrong? Questions to ask

1 Have I got spare cash to invest?
2 If so, is this the best use for it?
3 For what purpose is the company seeking to raise capital?
4 What is my view of the company's performance to date, and will the additional capital serve to improve performance?
5 Will the new capital work to increase profits and earnings? If not, with new shares in issue, existing shareholders will face 'dilution' – the same amount of dividends will be shared out more thinly.
6 How badly will the issue affect the share price? If the company is well regarded in the market, the price may not fall as much as the rights issue calculation might suggest.
7 Am I prepared to suffer the fall in share price without the compensation of taking up the rights issue?

Scrip issues

If a company's shares have been successfully trading on the stockmarket for a long time, and the price has become very high, the company may make a scrip issue (also known as a capitalisation, or bonus, issue).

A scrip issue has no material effect on the value of your shares: what happens is that you are offered extra free shares in proportion to your holding: 'one for one' or 'one for two', for instance.

The share price falls to take account of extra shares, so you end up with more shares, each worth less, but the value of your holding is the same. Say the share price is £12. The scrip issue is one for two. Two shares at £24, become three shares: the new share price is £8.

Perks

Shareholder perks – known more soberly as shareholder concessions – are discounts and other benefits derived from a company's business and made available to shareholders. Many famous name companies offer this sort of sweetener to investors: you can get cut-price channel crossings or football shirts, seats at sporting events, reductions on clothing, and money off your dry cleaning bill.

The best advice on this subject is: don't buy the stock just to get the perk. Perhaps this could be amended to: don't buy for the perk unless it is worth more to you than possible ups and downs in the share price.

There are, in any case, some caveats associated with perks:

❍ You usually need a minimum shareholding – perhaps 1,000 shares, in many instances – in order to qualify for the perk.

❍ Perks may even only be available to holders of a special class of share, or to founder shareholders in the case of a new issue.

❍ You should check the exact terms of the concession: is that discount on every purchase, or only on one purchase a year?

❍ There are some companies which will not allow you to take the concession if your shares are held through a nominee company. This means shares held in Personal Equity Plans as well, because PEPs always use nominees.

❍ It is impossible to generalise about the performance of companies offering perks. The list includes some high flyers as well as some poor performers (called 'dogs' by the professionals). The monetary value of the concession will probably take many years to equal the buying price of the shares, so don't get carried away. Make an extra effort to be objective when assessing companies which offer perks.

Buying abroad

THOUGH THIS BOOK is mainly about the UK stockmarket, shares from other countries may also be of interest to private investors.

There are various reasons why foreign shares can be attractive. For UK investors shares in any quoted EU company are eligible for tax-free PEP investment (see Chapter 7). Other countries may also have privatisation programmes – a trend which has caught the imagination of UK investors, and has made profits for many.

There may also be a degree of glamour and excitement in some overseas stocks. The US smaller companies market – NASDAQ – which has a reputation for fast-moving, high-tech stocks, has advertised in the UK.

How easy it is for the UK private investor to buy overseas stocks direct depends partly on the country. Companies from small Far Eastern markets, for example, may in practice be inaccessible to the private investor. Even fund managers use other funds to gain access to some of these markets. But for European stocks and stocks in other familiar, developed markets like the US, buying is not too difficult, though the costs of dealing may rule it out for all except the very big investor. Most stockbrokers will advise the use of unit trusts or investment trusts for overseas investment, even for those with very large investment portfolios.

If you are still enthusiastic about the overseas market, you can deal in foreign shares through many brokers. You may even be able to do it over the phone. But bear in mind there are numerous costs involved: commission from the UK broker and an agent broker in the country concerned; a custody charge; currency conversion and dividend collection charges; and other administrative costs. The overall charge could vary enormously between brokers, and it is worth checking prices with several. You could pay £250 to £350 for a £10,000 European purchase. Even then you should check carefully as to the terms of the custody arrangements.

European investors have tended historically to favour bonds rather than equities, so their share markets are not as well geared up to the private investor as the UK. This means a high minimum for share bargains. You might manage with a purchase size of £5,000, but £10,000 or £15,000 would be more comfortable.

The need for custodian arrangements in Europe is because share certificates are in 'bearer' form, so they cannot be replaced if they are lost. It is a necessity to have your shares held for you by a recognised custodian. Some states will not allow stock out of the country.

The other problem with overseas investment is research. Some brokers will have expertise in foreign markets, but it is very hard to research smaller and more interesting overseas companies yourself. This is one good reason to invest through a fund. There are both unit trusts and investment trusts which adopt quite a specialist approach to overseas investment, concentrating on a single smaller market or even on smaller companies with a market or markets.

If you look at a number of funds you may find one that covers the range of companies which interest you. But it pays to look in detail at several: a broker who analysed the contents of US smaller companies funds in early 1997 found that some had so much in NASDAQ as to be almost NASDAQ funds, while other funds from major management groups had no NASDAQ stocks at all.

Investing overseas: points to remember

1 Unless you have a high risk tolerance and plenty of money to invest, use funds for overseas investment.

2 Choose a broker with some expertise in the markets which interest you.

3 Shop around on price.

4 Check exactly on the terms offered: does the custody fee cover all holdings, or only one, for example?

5 Don't assume that all privatisations are successful. Some European issues have performed poorly compared to their UK counterparts.

6 Bear in mind that research into overseas companies will be difficult, and even checking prices daily could be problematic for some countries.

7 Look out for new funds offering specialist foreign opportunities.

Though a market like NASDAQ is in the high-risk category for a UK investor, it is at least relatively easy to find out about. NASDAQ has its own website which will even allow you to run a dummy portfolio and see how you get on. Costs for dealing in this market could be lower than for European countries, but you should still expect to invest a high minimum.

Action plan

○ Unless you are confident, approach your decision on whether or not to buy new issues like any other shares.

○ If you receive warrants with new issues, don't just forget about them – you may need to get advice on what to do with them, and when.

○ If a company in which you own shares is the target of a takeover bid, make sure you keep up to date with progress and follow the checklist on page 68 – establish your best option.

○ If a company in which you own shares has a rights issue, follow our checklist (page 68) to decide whether to take up the offer.

○ Don't buy shares just for the perks, but don't miss out on the perks from companies in which you own shares.

○ If you're interested in buying shares abroad, bear in mind that costs can be high, minimum investments can be high, and it can be hard to get the information you need.

BEING A SHAREHOLDER

71

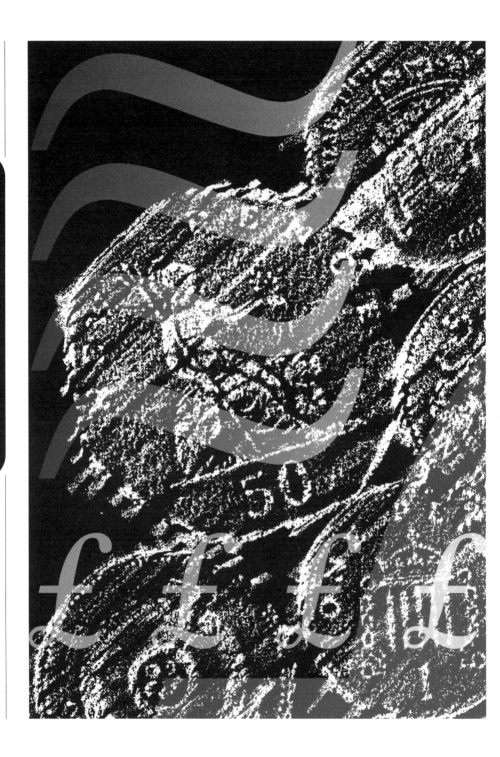

5 Unit trusts

Unit trusts are the ideal way for small investors to get into the stockmarket. You can invest in a wide range of sectors from as little as £50 a month.

The main advantages of unit trusts are:
- You can invest with relatively small amounts of money.
- The risk is spread and therefore reduced because each unit represents a proportion of a big fund, which in itself holds a large portfolio of different stocks.

Launched in the UK in the 1930s, the unit trust industry today manages £151bn of private investors' money. There are currently almost 150 unit trust groups managing a total of 1,700 unit trust funds.

The best performing unit trusts have been successful in giving good stockmarket returns to investors. The table on page 74 shows how much you would have made by investing a £1,000 lump sum or £50 a month in average funds in the major unit trust sectors over five, ten and fifteen years.

Apart from the risk of markets falling, the unit trust industry has remained remarkably free of risk to investors through fraud, negligence or the collapse of management groups. Scandals have occurred, but either unitholders' funds have been ringfenced and therefore unaffected (as with the Barings scandal of 1995), or the fund manager's parent organisation has stepped in to make good any damage (as Deutsche Bank did in 1996 for Morgan Grenfell). This is one good reason to choose a fund management group backed by a large and reputable organisation.

HOW A UNIT TRUST WORKS

The flowchart on page 77 provides a summary. As its name indicates, it is a trust. It has a trustee, usually a high-street bank, which owns and is responsible for the safe-keeping of the investments, and a unitholder, who is the beneficiary. The trust takes the form of a fund, which holds a number of investments, chosen and managed (that is, monitored day to day and changed as necessary)

UNIT TRUST PERFORMANCE

Average performance of the major unit trust sectors compared to a building society and to the Retail Price Index (RPI).

	£1,000 lump sum *			£50 a month **		
	5 yrs £	10 yrs £	15 yrs £	5 yrs £	10 yrs £	15 yrs £
UK Growth & Income	1,883	2,218	9,851	4,110	10,529	26,786
UK Growth	1,908	2,048	9,260	4,171	10,676	25,984
UK Equity Income	1,894	2,212	10,472	4,071	10,504	27,576
Europe	2,220	2,750	14,080	4,521	12,307	32,208
Far East excl Japan	2,194	3,168	8,952	3,724	12,801	32,274
Japan	1,504	1,230	7,131	2,886	6,240	15,988
Nth America	2,548	2,975	8,811	4,533	13,713	27,397
Building Society	1,178	1,764	2,622	3,287	7,665	14,231
RPI	1,126	1,540	1,922	3,273	7,268	12,468
All-Share Index	2,122	2,675	11,223	4,556	12,499	30,955

* Redemption value of £1,000 lump sum; ** £50 a month invested over 5, 10 and 15 years to 1.7.97, offer-to-bid, net income reinvested

Source: AUTIF (Association of Unit Trusts and Investment Funds)

by the fund manager. The fund manager, under the watchful eye of his or her employer, the trustee, also markets the unit trust to the public, sells units to individual investors and buys them back again when the investor wants to redeem his or her holding.

When investors want to buy units the fund manager asks the trustee to create them. When investors sell units back the fund manager can either sell them on to other investors who want to buy, or ask the trustee to void or 'liquidate' them.

Because of this ability to create and liquidate units, a unit trust, is described as an 'open-ended' fund, unlike an investment trust which has a fixed number of shares in issue.

Both the fund manager and the trustee make a charge for their services, and these are built in to the price of the units.

The unit price itself may rise and fall in line with the stock-market value of the fund's investments, creating a gain or a loss for the investor. The trust may also pay out dividends, which provide the investor with an income.

Unit trusts have two prices:

○ The offer price is the price at which the manager offers units to the public – the buying price from the investor's point of view.

○ The bid price is what the manager bids to buy units back – the investor's selling price.

The difference between the two prices is called the spread. Unlike share prices, which are fixed by the market, unit trust prices depend on a calculation according to a statutory formula. The system is quite complicated (see page 90).

Independent financial adviser and *Moneywise* Ask the Professionals panellist Brian Dennehy says:

"Steady household names, rollercoaster emerging markets, squeaky clean ethical, or long-term income generation – whatever your investment objective, and however you want to achieve it, unit trusts provide plenty of opportunities."

WHERE YOU CAN INVEST

Today you can invest through unit trusts in an enormous range of markets, from Chile to China. Unit trusts can also invest in government securities (gilts) and other very safe fixed-interest instruments, while money-market unit trusts can invest in deposits which simply pay interest, but at a higher rate than your high-street bank. Altogether, there are now 25 different unit trust categories as defined by the Association of Unit Trusts and Investment Funds (AUTIF), which is the fund managers' trade association (see sector listing on pages 78 and 79).

SOME SPECIAL TYPES OF FUND

○ *Index tracker trusts*: Tracker trusts were first launched on the principle that few unit trusts beat the stockmarket index over the long term, and many poorer performers often do much worse than the market as a whole. A trust which could track or mirror the performance of the index should therefore be among the best performing funds over a number of years and would remove the risk of choosing a poor performer.

Tracker funds use a number of complex, computer-based systems to track accurately the relevant index. The computer effectively tells the fund manager what to buy and sell. These funds are therefore known as 'passive' funds, in contrast to 'active' funds, where the manager has to do all the research and arrive at his or her own stock selections.

Passive fund management is criticised by active fund managers, who say that their aim is to outperform the index, not just to shadow it. In practice an index fund will always perform slightly below the index, because of the effect of charges. But index tracker funds are now proving their worth as relatively low-risk core holdings.

○ *Ethical trusts*: Like tracker trusts, ethical and 'green' unit trusts were met initially with some scepticism. These trusts filter their investments according to a number of criteria. For example, they may not invest in companies which deal in arms, drugs or alcohol; which test products on animals; which trade with oppressive regimes or which pollute the environment.

The exact ethical and environmental criteria used vary between funds. You should should check on the individual fund's approach.

Many investors find the ethical approach attractive, but mainstream investment experts complain that it rules out a large number of strong companies, and so prevents the fund from achieving top-rank performance. But the ethical sector has proved that it can produce good performance, although some funds have been more successful than others.

Ethical funds tend to hold a higher than usual percentage of small companies, so they may have a higher risk profile than a conventional unit trust.

○ *Guaranteed or protected trusts*: Both types of fund are another attempt by the industry to provide for the cautious or inexperienced investor. These trusts undertake to return the

How a unit trust works

REGULATORS

SIB
Writes the rules.

PIA
Monitors marketing of units.

IMRO
Monitors all other aspects of
unit trust management.

UNIT TRUST MANAGER
• Launches trust.
• Markets trust.
• Manages trust.
• Asks trustee to create
and liquidate units.
• Values and calculates
price of units.
• Buys and sells to public.

INVESTOR
• Beneficial owner
of trust fund.
• Buys units.
• Sells units.
• Switches funds.

TRUSTEE
• Legal owner of fund assets.
• Creates and liquidates units.
• Holds securities on behalf
of trust.
• Holds income and pays
it out.
•Makes sure trust is managed
within terms of trust deed.
• Has oversight of pricing and
investment and borrowing
powers, making sure trust is
run within regulations.
• Responsible for unitholder
registration (keeping track of
who holds units). In practice,
this task is usually done by
the manager or a separate
registrar.

Guide to the unit trust sectors

KEY

£ = low/no yield
££ = moderate yields
£££ = high yields
$/! = overseas currency risk

! = low risk
!! = moderate risk
!!! = high risk
!!!! = very high risk

I = good for income investors
G = good for growth investors

UK

Growth & Income:
At least 80% in the UK. Yield 80%–110% of FT-A All-Share Index.
Moneywise rating: Lower risk than a pure growth fund. **££ !! I G**

Equity Income:
At least 80% UK equities. Yield 110%+ that of FT-A All-Share Index.
Moneywise rating: Exposed to equity market risks, but should be less volatile than growth sector. **££ !! I G**

Growth:
At least 80% UK equities.
Moneywise rating: **£ !!! G**

Smaller Companies:
At least 80% UK companies in Hoare Govett UK Smaller Companies Extended Index.
Moneywise rating: **£ !!! G**

Gilts:
At least 80% in UK gilts.
Moneywise rating: Growth possibilities limited. **£££ ! I**

Other Fixed Interest:
At least 80% in UK corporate or public fixed interest.
Moneywise rating: **£££ ! I**

Equity & Bond:
At least 80% UK; less than 80% equities or fixed interest.
Moneywise rating: **££ ! I**

Equity & Bond Income:
Yield 120% that of FTSEAA Index.
Moneywise rating: **£££ ! I**

INTERNATIONAL

Growth:
At least 80% equities.
Moneywise rating: International portfolios not relying on a single market. Asset allocation will be an important element for fund's success. **£ !!! G $/!**

Equity Income:
At least 80% equities. Yield 110% of FT Actuaries World Index.
Moneywise rating: **££ !!! I $/!**

Fixed Interest:
At least 80% fixed interest. Includes all non-UK fixed interest funds.
Moneywise rating: Funds may be international or confined to one market. Growth possibilities limited. **£££ !! I $/!**

Equity & Bond:
At least 80% in either equities or fixed interest.
Moneywise rating: **££ !! I G $/!**

SPECIALIST INTERNATIONAL SECTORS

Japan:
At least 80% in Japan.
Moneywise rating: Sector may include blue chip, smaller company or specialist funds – risk varies. **£ !!! G $/!**

Far East, including Japan:
At least 80% Far East. May be up to 80% in Japan.
Moneywise rating: **£ !!!! G $/!**

Far East, excluding Japan:
As above, but with no Japan content.
Moneywise rating: **£ !!!! G $/!**

North America:
At least 80% in the US.
Moneywise rating: May include blue chip, smaller company or specialist funds. **£ !!! G $/!**

Europe:
At least 80% in Europe (includes the UK, but not more than 80% UK.
Moneywise rating: Risk levels will vary – may include smaller companies funds. **£ !!! G $/!**

Global Emerging Markets:
At least 80% in emerging markets as defined by the World Bank.
Moneywise rating: The most risky category of funds. **£ !!!! G $/!**

SPECIALIST SECTORS REGARDLESS OF GEOGRAPHICAL MARKETS

Commodity & Energy:
At least 80% in commodity and energy sectors.
Moneywise rating: Small sector, largely gold funds. **£ !!!! G $/!**

Property:
At least 80% in property companies.
Moneywise rating: Highly specialist funds. Mostly UK. **££ !!! G**

Investment Trust Units:
Only hold investment trust shares.
Moneywise rating: UK shares, but funds may invest overseas. **£ !!! G**

Funds of Funds:
Only hold other unit trusts.
Moneywise rating: Mostly managed portfolios of unit trusts. **£ !!! G**

Money market:
At least 80% in deposit investments.
Moneywise rating: May be used to hold cash pending investment. **£££ ! I**

Index Bear Funds:
Derivatives funds which inversely track market indices.
Moneywise rating: Very high risk – only for the expert investor. **££ !!! G I**

There is also a special trust sector for funds used in pension plans.

investor's original capital after a specified period, even if the market has fallen.

Guaranteed trusts are able to do this by having a guarantee provided by a third party, a factor which results in extra cost. The guarantee is only valid over a specific term (typically five years) and the trust usually has a limited open period for purchases.

Protected trusts use futures and options to limit losses (see Chapter 8). They are cheaper than guaranteed trusts, and the protection element works quarterly instead of over a period of years. Units can be bought and sold at any time.

○ *Broker trusts*: Broker unit trusts are run by investment advisers for their own clients. The manager of the fund is an established fund manager, who technically contracts out the management of the assets to the adviser concerned. The fund is normally known by the adviser's name.

The problem with broker trusts is the charges involved. Because the fund manager and the broker both take their remuneration from the fund, and there may also be charges attached to the underlying investments, the overall charges tend to be high.

○ *Funds of funds*: The concept is largely self-explanatory: funds of funds are unit trusts which invest in other unit trusts to provide a portfolio of different investments. A number of broker unit trusts are funds of funds, but the concept is also used by fund managers wishing to offer a managed fund based on their own trusts.

LATEST DEVELOPMENTS

A new type of fund was launched in 1997, designed to offer a simpler structure than the traditional unit trust. Open-ended company funds (OEICs) are similar to unit trusts in many respects.

A key difference between the two, however, is their pricing mechanism, in that only one price is quoted for OEICs, compared to the two prices (bid and offer price) published for unit trusts. It is possible that many existing unit trusts will switch to OEIC status. But it seems unlikely for the time being that OEICs will replace units.

The return

IF YOU ARE A UNIT TRUST INVESTOR there are two types of return you may get from your investment: income and growth.

You may get income from the trust distribution, which is comparable to the dividend on shares. You can opt to take the income from your units, in which case it is paid out to you, or you can reinvest it so that it can be used to buy further units.

Growth comes from an increase in the unit price. All unit trusts go up and down in price to a certain extent, so there may be periods when you see no growth, or when you may actually register a loss. But over the long term (five to ten years) you should see a rise again in unit values.

As with investment trusts (see Chapter 6), you can invest in unit trusts either with a lump sum or with regular monthly contributions. A typical minimum lump sum investment is £1,000, although there are still a number of groups that will accept £500.

A big advantage of unit trusts over shares is the regular savings option. Most unit trust groups offer a regular savings plan with a low monthly minimum. A few plans still allow you to invest with as little as £20 or £25 a month, but many nowadays state a minimum of £30 or £50, and some £100. The table on page 82 illustrates performance for both types of investment.

In theory the lump sum investor should have an advantage over the regular saver, since the lump sum buys a large number of units at the outset, whereas the regular saver only buys a few each month.

But the regular saver benefits from a statistical anomaly known as pound cost averaging. This boosts performance in general and can mean in certain market conditions that a small monthly contribution will produce a better result than the same total amount invested as a lump sum. Pound cost averaging works simply because the monthly contribution buys more units when the price is low than when it is high.

Boosted by pound cost averaging, regular saving in unit trusts has various advantages:

○ It is a form of protection against the downs of the unit trust price graph.

Example

Two neighbours decide to invest in the same unit trust. One has a lump sum of £1,200. The other puts in £100 a month for a year. They pick a volatile trust in a year of market ups and downs, as the price record shows. Because the price of their units falls and then recovers over the year, the regular saver ends up with more units – and therefore a more valuable holding – than the neighbour who invested the lump sum at the outset.

If the unit price had risen steadily during the year the lump sum investor would have done better than the regular saver, but pound cost averaging will always act to give the regular saver a boost when unit prices are falling.

	Price of units (pence)	£100 Monthly saver buys (units)	£1,200 lump sum buys (units)
January	100	100	1,200
February	90	111	
March	85	118	
April	85	118	
May	78	128	
June	82	122	
July	85	118	
August	88	114	
September	90	111	
October	105	95	
November	107	93	
December	110	91	
Total units:		1,319	1,200
Total value at end December:		£1,450.90	£1,320.00

○ It removes the need for investment timing decisions. By contrast, lump sum investments can be disastrous if they are made just before a crash.
○ It automatically means that you buy more units when the prices are low and fewer when the prices are high.
○ It reduces risk by spreading investment timing and by putting only small amounts at a time into the market.

Independent financial adviser and *Moneywise* Ask the professionals panellist Brian Dennehy says:

"Assessing unit trust performance is a problem because investors (and advisers!) put a portfolio of trusts together based on their long-term objectives, then judge performance of individual trusts over short periods. You must assess individual fund performance over longer rolling periods, and against the objectives of the fund manager and the way in which he or she intended to achieve this objective."

PERFORMANCE

Most published performance tables show results in cumulative form, that is, they show how growth has accumulated over a stated period to a particular cut-off date.

This is fine if you just want to see what your return would have been at the end of the period, but it tells you nothing about what happened in between. For example, if there is a dramatic movement in price near the end of the period, the cumulative figure you see may not represent the fund's performance throughout the period.

One way to get a better idea of performance consistency is to look at figures for discrete periods – that is, year on year, or during one sixth-monthly period after another. Graphs give a better overall view of performance, although the actual results may be harder to read.

SOME POPULAR PERFORMANCE THEORIES

○ *Small funds do better than large funds*: The theory is that small funds are more 'agile' than large funds and so are more able to turn in a good performance. It is true that small funds can sometimes perform very strongly. They have relatively few holdings and if one or two of their investments do very well, the effect on the fund is dramatic. Likewise, their performance can be dragged down if one or two stocks fail.

There are a number of very large funds whose performance has been indifferent, but the most competent management groups have proved that this need not always be the case. Investors should look at performance history, not just size, before deciding on a fund.

○ *New funds do better than old funds*: The idea here is that a new fund has a fresh impetus and is not weighed down by a lot of dead wood in the portfolio. New funds seem to be very attractive to investors in marketing terms, so this idea is one that unit trust advisers are happy to foster.

Judging performance

○ Net income reinvested. Most perfor-mance figures shown are net income reinvested, that is, they assume that dividends net of basic rate tax have been used to buy more units. Figures like this show ...

○ Total return. This is growth and reinvested income combined. It is possible for total return figures to mask poor capital growth where a fund has a high yield. Check growth and income performance separately if you are looking at this type of fund.

○ Gross income reinvested. This is what you get with PEPs, so net fig-ures will show an underperformance.

○ Performance figures will usually be offer-to-bid, that is, the initial price is the offer price, and the end price is the bid price. This means the calcula-tion is comparable to a purchase and sale. Occasionally, figures are shown offer-to-offer, which will enhance them by the amount of the bid/offer spread (see page 90).

○ Quartile rankings. These show where the fund lies within its sector. First quartile means it is in the top 25%, and so on. Look for funds that are consistently in the first and second quartiles over different periods.

○ Top tens. Fund managers love to promote successful funds. Remember that a fund which has been number one in a single year is unlikely to repeat this performance. Go for funds that are consistently good, not momentarily outstanding.

○ Picking the worst. One investment theory suggests that you should choose the worst performer, on the grounds that it must do better next year. This works occasionally, but is not to be relied on as a regular strategy.

○ Performance sectors (see guide to unit trust sectors, pages 78 and 79). All the funds in one sector should have the same broad investment cri-teria to help you compare like with like. You will not get a true picture if you compare a small technology com-panies trust with a blue chip fund.

○ Finding a benchmark. Compare your fund to a relevant measure – its sec-tor, its market index, the building society, inflation – whatever seems most relevant in your circumstances.

Like small funds, new funds may or may not make good. From the investor's point of view, they lack a performance pedigree on which to base a judgement. Choosing a new fund will always carry a greater risk than deciding on an established one, though a new Far East fund from a group which has already had great success in that market will be a safer bet than a similar fund from a new management group, or from a group whose reputation so far has been founded in UK income funds.

○ *If a good fund manager leaves then it's time to sell your units:* Unit trust advisers certainly put a lot of weight on the fund manager's performance record, and if a manager moves to a new group, many advisers will follow. For the private investor, the value of this theory is hard to assess. If the fund is highly specialised, and its management is strongly dependent on the flair of one individual, the moment that individual leaves may be the time to get out. If the management group's success is built on team effort and a well-defined house investment philosophy, the loss of an individual should not spell disaster. Such groups, interestingly, tend also to be better at keeping their top managers.

INVESTING FOR INCOME

Like stockmarket companies, unit trusts usually pay income to investors twice yearly. Some unit trusts, where the emphasis is on income, pay quarterly. Others, where dividends are low, may pay only once a year. A handful pay out monthly.

The rate paid by the fund is called the yield. It is the fund's prospective annual income expressed as a percentage of the offer price. So a unit trust priced at 60p and paying 2·4p per unit would have a 4% yield.

Some unit trusts aim to pay a high income. Others concentrate on producing growth in the unit price, and invest in companies where dividends may be low or non-existent. Most overseas funds have low or zero distributions, as do most smaller companies funds.

The manager of an income fund will do his or her best to maintain dividends at a constant level, or to increase them. Since dividends depend on the business fortunes of the companies in the fund, this is harder to do in some years than in others.

EXAMPLE
An investor buys 1,000 units at £1 each. The yield is 3%, so in the first year she receives £30. After ten years the units are worth £2 each and the yield has been maintained at 3%. The investor now has assets worth £2,000 and receives distributions worth £60 (3% x £2,000) in the year. Five years later the unit price has again gone up, to £2·50. The yield has also increased to 3·5%. The investor's holding is now worth £2,500 and her income is £87·50.

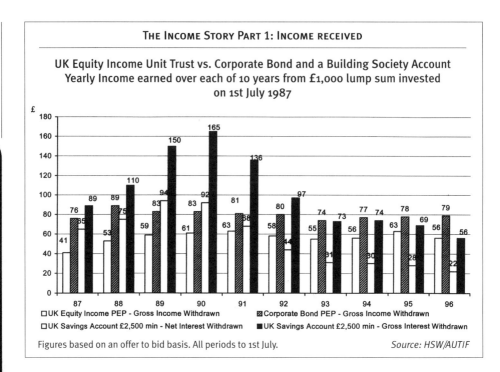

THE INCOME STORY PART 1: INCOME RECEIVED

UK Equity Income Unit Trust vs. Corporate Bond and a Building Society Account
Yearly Income earned over each of 10 years from £1,000 lump sum invested
on 1st July 1987

□ UK Equity Income PEP - Gross Income Withdrawn   ▨ Corporate Bond PEP - Gross Income Withdrawn
□ UK Savings Account £2,500 min - Net Interest Withdrawn   ■ UK Savings Account £2,500 min - Gross Interest Withdrawn

Figures based on an offer to bid basis. All periods to 1st July.   *Source: HSW/AUTIF*

Over the long term the best income funds have an excellent record of maintaining growth in distributions. So although the yield on a unit trust may be low initially, and not guaranteed to stay at the same level, income funds have great attractions for those who can afford to wait.

The example reflects the dual growth that an income unit trust can produce. The bar chart above shows average figures for a UK equity income PEP compared to a corporate bond PEP (see Chapter 7) and an interest-paying savings account over ten years to July 1997.

The chart shows that the income from the savings account, dependent on interest rates, has gone up and down a lot over the period. In 1996 it was returning almost 40% less than in 1987. The equity PEP,

BEST OF ALL WORLDS
An older female investor seeks a balanced, relatively low-risk investment in unit trusts, with a reasonable level of income. Her adviser recommends that she place her money in a portfolio made up of 50% equity funds, 40% fixed-interest and 10% money-market funds. This combination of funds makes the best use of all the sectors, giving long-term growth possibilities as well as a higher yield than she would get with a straight equity portfolio.

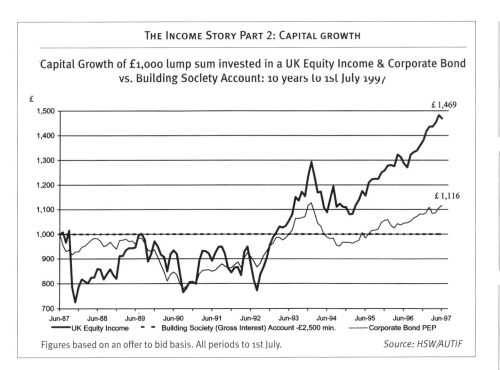

THE INCOME STORY PART 2: CAPITAL GROWTH

Capital Growth of £1,000 lump sum invested in a UK Equity Income & Corporate Bond vs. Building Society Account: 10 years to 1st July 1997

£ 1,469

£ 1,116

UK Equity Income — Building Society (Gross Interest) Account -£2,500 min. — Corporate Bond PEP

Figures based on an offer to bid basis. All periods to 1st July.   *Source: HSW/AUTIF*

while not equalling the returns of 1989–1991, when interest rates were very high, produced reasonable steady growth, with returns of 6·7% in 1996 – almost 40% higher than the starting yield. Corporate bonds also produced steady yields, with 1996 returning a little more than 1987.

The graph shows the capital growth side of the story. It is here the equity fund wins hands down, with a £1,000 initial investment growing to £1,469 over the period. Total return on the three investments were £2,502 (equity PEP), £2,336 (corporate bond PEP) and £2,018 (interest-paying account).

Investors who want to receive distributions as they are paid should ask for income units. If they want the income to be reinvested they should buy accumulation units.

Unit trusts that invest in shares (equity unit trusts) are not the only type of fund which offers an income. Income-seeking investors should also look at fixed-interest and money-market funds.

○ Fixed-interest funds invest in gilts (UK government stocks) and other types of bond paying a fixed return (see Chapter 8).

Fixed-interest funds designed for income can offer yields substantially higher than those of equity funds but they do not offer the possibilities for growth of an equity income fund, and both the yield and capital value can fall.

○ Money-market funds pay an interest rate return just like from a building society account, though the rates such funds offer are likely to be higher than those of a building society.

INCOME FOR GROWTH

Income funds are not only for the income investor. UK Equity income funds have such a good historic record of growth that they are widely used by investors as a steady and relatively low-risk element in general equity portfolios.

The income fund discipline is partly what underlies the income fund's success. Income fund managers invest in companies which are paying good dividends, and whose prospects for dividend growth look good. If the company does well and its share price goes up significantly, it will not be able to maintain its initial high yield. In order for the yield on the fund to remain unaffected, the manager must sell the investment and start again with another promising company which looks cheaper. In other words, the fund buys companies which are cheap and sells them when they become expensive – a classic recipe for successful growth investment.

REGULAR INCOME FROM FUNDS
A friend of the older female investor (page 86) needs to concentrate on growth with a small income boost from her £30,000 savings, but she needs a monthly income. The same adviser suggests a regular income portfolio, which uses six different unit trust income funds, each paying twice yearly in different months. Though the income in each month is not exactly the same, the combination – which could be set up by any investor on his or her own behalf – provides a neat solution to this particular investor's income needs, which may increase as time goes on.

Investing for income

Do you or will you need income from your savings to live on?

Yes → **No**

Yes branch

Which is closer to your situation?

- **I need to supplement my income immediately.**
  - Depending on the level of income needed, look at equity income or bond funds or a combination of the two.

- **I need to supplement my income later on.**
  - Choose a medium-yield income fund and reinvest the income. Switch to taking income as the need arises.

- **I need a maximum immediate boost to income.**
  - Are you under 65?
    - Equity income funds may not yield enough for your needs but bond funds offer little prospect of growth to keep up with inflation. Providing for both will depend on your other assets. Take advice.
  - Are you 65 or over?
    - You could consider bond or fixed-interest funds but should also look at high-yielding options outside unit trusts such as gilts, PIBs and annuities.

No branch

- **Do you already have a core portfolio and want a more specialist fund?**
  - Income funds are not for you.

- **Are you looking for a steady, general fund, a core fund as a basis for savings, or a good general fund for a PEP?**
  - Income funds are well suited to all these purposes.

UNIT TRUSTS

89

How to buy and sell

THE SYSTEM FOR PRICING units is actually quite complicated, but you won't necessarily need to get to grips with the detail. This is the way it works.

Fund managers:
○ Take the current market value of shares in the fund.
○ Add stamp duty (see Chapter 9), stockbrokers' commissions and an amount representing income accrued since the last distribution to give the creation price (the amount the manager pays the trustee to create units).
○ Add the manager's initial charge and perhaps an amount for rounding to give the maximum issue price or full offer price – the highest price at which the manager is allowed to sell units.

The bid price calculation (the manager's buying price) is the same process in reverse:
○ Value the portfolio as before.
○ Take away commission and accrued income to give the bid price – the price the trustee will pay the manager when units are cancelled, or the cancellation price – the lowest price the manager can pay when redeeming units.

Between the maximum offer price and the minimum bid price the spread could be quite high – higher, perhaps, than would be acceptable in the market. So managers usually set a spread inside the upper and lower limits, typically of around 6%.

If demand for units is strong, fund managers may set the offer price (the investor's buying price) at its highest limit, but raise the bid price to reduce the spread. This is called trading on an offer price basis.

If the manager is trying to stimulate interest by keeping the price of units low, he or she will reduce the offer price, perhaps keeping the bid price at its lowest level. In this case, the trust is on a bid price basis.

Most investors do not wish to get involved in the complications of pricing, though it may be of interest to the experienced investor who wants to get an idea of whether units are cheap or expensive. The simplest way to find out is to phone and ask the dealers.

AUTHORISED INVESTMENT FUNDS -

Unit Trusts and OEICs

(Open-ended investment companies).

Name and address of management group. Phone number for dealing

Time of valuation and whether dealing is forward (**F**) or historic (**H**)

Offer price

Initial charge

Gross yield (ie without any deduction for tax). All funds show a yield, even when none is actually paid

Bid price
Price 'xd' means the fund is trading ex-distribution

	Init Chrge	Notes	Selling Price	Buying Price	+ or -	Yield Gr's

ABN AMRO Pembroke Ltd (0800)F
37–41 Bedford Row, London WC1R 4JH.   0171–813 2244

UK Growth	5		261.99	278.71	+2.61	1.21
World	6		100.73	107.16	+0.22	0.54
Balanced	5	C	218.92	232.89	+1.20	3.45
Equity Income	5	C	139.24	147.34	+0.64	5.17
High Income	5	C	53.00	56.38	−0.06	7.99

AIB Govett Unit Trusts Limited (1000)F
Shackleton House, 4 Battlebridge Lane, London SE1 2HR
0171–378 7979   Dealing: 0171–407 7888

Protected Funds

UK Safeguard	5½		138.790xd	147.890	+0.21	0.00
Do ;fixed minimum NAV to Sept 19⁹			129.82	129.82	.....	−
UK Equity Safeguard Acc	5½		108.36	115.82	−0.1	2.47
Do [Fixed Maximum NAV to Sep 19⁹	5½		101.73	101.73	.....	−
Cash ♦	½		£9.5609xd	9.6087	.....	5.75

UK Growth Funds

UK Equity General	5		357.40xd	380.20	+2.00	1.74
British Growth	5½		82.42	88.14	.....	1.43
UK Small Co's	5½		76.20xd	81.49	.....	0.49
FTSE 250 Index	5½		96.62	103.32	+0.4	2.11
Geared UK Index	5½		£22.7307xd	24.0596	+0.23	5.25

Income Funds

UK Equity Inc	5½	C	111.30xd	119.03	+0.1	4.24
Corporate Bond	3¼		79.20	81.82	−0.01	0.00
Monthly Income	5½		42.40xd	45.23	.....	8.47

International Funds

American General	5		305.80	323.60	−1.1	0.00
American Strategy	5½		279.19	298.59	−0.1	0.00
JG US Index ♦	5¼		£23.369xd	24.6236	.....	4.00
European General	5		333.70	352.80	+0.2	0.64
European Strategy	5½		147.21	157.44	+0.1	0.00
Japan General	5		130.80	138.40	−0.1	0.00
Japan Strategy	5½		44.65	47.10	−0.4	0.00
Asia Pacific	5		91.74	98.02	−0.65	0.00
Pacific Strategy	5½		154.63	165.37	.....	0.00
Greater China	5½		310.13	331.69	−4.3	0.00
Latin America	5½		128.85	137.79	+1.7	0.00
Intl Growth	5½		183.52	196.27	.....	0.00
Balanced Exempt	3		152.90	158.40	.....	2.26
Global Strategy	5½		51.77	55.36	−0.22	0.00

Unit trusts are valued every day at a specific time known as the valuation point. The price arrived at will be used for all sales during that valuation period. Fund managers can either buy and sell at the price to be fixed at the next valuation point (forward pricing) or at the price fixed at the last valuation point (historic pricing).

Most groups deal on a forward pricing basis, and a lot have 12 noon as their valuation point. Deals made in the morning before 12 are therefore priced at the same day's noon valuation. A deal made at 12.05pm would be valued at noon on the following day. This means that almost 24 hours pass before the price is fixed, which could cause problems if markets fall sharply in the meantime.

If dealings are on a historic basis the fund manager must switch to forward dealing:

○ If asked to do so by the purchaser.
○ If the fund value is thought to have moved by more than 2% since the last valuation.
○ For very large deals.

The point behind the offer and bid calculation is to ensure that the costs of creating or cancelling units are fairly apportioned to unitholders coming into or going out of the fund, rather than being borne by the fund itself, and hence by existing investors.

Forward pricing was introduced as part of changes brought about by the Financial Services Act, so that investors could be sure that they were buying and selling at fair prices. Under the old historic system managers could, for example, create units in the afternoon at today's price, knowing that the market had risen and those units could be sold to investors the next day at an instant profit.

The panel on page 91 shows how unit trust prices appear in the national press (in this instance from the *Financial Times*).

You can buy unit trusts directly as the box on page 93 shows, or you might decide you need advice.

Independent financial adviser and *Moneywise* Ask the Professionals panellist Rebekah Kearey says:

"Many unit trust providers offer a service whereby all or part of your investment portfolio can be exchanged for units in their unit trusts. The costs are usually much lower than if you sold your shares through a stockbroker, but you are unable to stipulate the timing of the sale. The minimum deal size is often quite large – £10,000 or higher is not unusual, but some companies will exchange holdings as small as £500."

How to buy and sell: a step-by-step guide

1 **PHONE THE UNIT TRUST GROUP'S DEALERS OR FAX THEM IF YOU PREFER** Dealers' phone numbers can be found in the press, where the group's prices are quoted. The dealers can give you basic information about the trust but they cannot advise.

2 **PLACE YOUR ORDER** You can either ask for a number of units or say: 'I want £1,000 worth...'. If dealing is historic the dealer can give you the price. Otherwise you will have to wait until you get your contract note in the post to find out how much you have paid per unit.

3 **THE CONTRACT NOTE ARRIVES** You should receive your contract note within two days. Check the details carefully on receipt, in case of error. Any disagreement should be pursued promptly. Management groups usually tape phone conversations with dealers.

4 **FILE THE CONTRACT NOTE CAREFULLY** The contract note is your only proof of ownership. If the management group you are buying from still uses certificates, you will get them by post some weeks later.

5 **PAYMENT FOR THE UNITS** This is due when you receive the contract note.

6 **SELLING UNITS CAN BE DONE BY PHONE IN THE SAME WAY** In most cases you will need to fill in the renunciation form on the contract note and return it to the management group before you can receive payment.

○ *Taking advice:* A lot of unit trust business is done through financial advisers. They may be stockbrokers or independent financial advisers (IFAs). It is important to check your adviser's commission terms. Some will share the commission element of the front-end charge with the client, especially one dealing in large amounts. A small number of advisers will charge a fee for advice and rebate all the commissions they receive. Solicitors and accountants are most likely to work like this.

○ *Share exchange:* Many managers run share exchange schemes to allow investors with a share portfolio to swap it for unit trusts. This is useful for clients who may have inherited shares or for those who feel they want the relatively lower risk of funds. The fund manager will take over the shares and either sell them or absorb them into its funds.

The terms on which share exchange is offered are usually better than if the investor went to a stockbroker to realise his or her cash. The unit trust manager might pay the dealing costs on the transaction, for example.

Share exchange may only be available on large amounts, and terms are more likely to be good for well-known blue chip shares than for obscure smaller companies. If you are making a substantial investment it is worth negotiating with the management group. Good terms on a share exchange scheme could equate to a worthwhile discount on the purchase of units.

Q&A

Q Do unit trusts go ex-dividend, like shares?

A Yes. They go ex-distribution (xd) about six weeks before the distribution is paid, after which the next dividend goes to the seller, not the buyer. The price of the units falls when the trust goes xd to reflect the removal of the accrued income from the price.

Q I have found the term 'equalisation' on my first dividend statement. What does it mean?

A If you buy units in the middle of a distribution period, you will pay the unit price for all the income accrued to date even prior to when you held the units. Equalisation is a refund of capital to make up for this 'overpayment'. As such it is not taxable as income and can be deducted from the cost of the investment for capital gains tax purposes.

Q Can I cancel a purchase of units?

A You have the right to cancel your unit trust purchase within 14 days, but only if you received advice on the transaction (this is to protect investors against pressure selling or inappropriate advice). The unit trust group will send you a form, which you can sign and return if you want to cancel. You do not get cancellation rights on execution-only deals: those which were done direct with the unit trust group.

Cancellation does not imply that you get your investment back in full. If the market falls between the date of the purchase and the date of cancellation, the amount you get back will reflect the fall. You should also remember that, confusingly, the cancellation price of units is not the price you get when you cancel. In practice investors rarely, if ever, take up cancellation rights.

Q *What are discount brokers?*

A Discount brokers will take your order on an execution-only basis and pass on most of their commission, giving a substantial discount on the unit price. This is OK if you have a good idea of what you should buy, but if you are uncertain, it will pay in the long run to forgo the discount and seek advice. Discount brokers advertise widely in the press.

Q *Can I get special terms if I switch within the same group's funds?*

A Yes, usually. Most groups offer switching discounts, which could be up to 4%. If you intend to switch, it is important to mention switching discount when you give your instructions to the dealers, as groups may not offer it automatically. If you insist a little, you may be able to improve on the deal.

  If you deal through an adviser it is also important to establish in advance what his or her terms are. Some advisers will pass on the bulk of the switching discount. Others will only pass on part of it.

Q *My mother has some unit certificates dated 1982. The trust concerned is no longer listed in the prices pages. How can I trace it?*

A Takeovers and mergers are a common problem for unitholders, who find themselves unexpectedly holding units in a different fund to the one they started out with. Any corporate action concerning your holdings will be notified to you when it happens. Keep the documents filed with your other unit trust papers to remind you.

  Mergers may occur within a management group because a fund has performed poorly, or, if the management group is taken over by another company, the combined list of funds may contain two with the same investment objective.

  Fund mergers do not involve the unitholder in any cost, nor is any action required except to take note of the merger and file the documents relating to it. There is no capital gains tax liability when holdings from the old trust are transferred into the new one.

Tracing an old trust is more problematic. There are two publications which list most fund changes for the last twenty years or so. They are: *UK Fund Industry Review and Directory* and the *Unit Trust Year Book* – these are expensive publications so try your local library.

Q *How can ordinary investors get hold of some of the more technical information about unit trusts?*

A Unit trust groups themselves are helpful if you address queries directly to them. Full listings of prices are given in the national press, and there are specialist publications and data services which give further information. There are more details in the Directory at the end of the book.

○ *Charges*: There are two types of charge on a unit trust: the initial charge and the annual management charge. The initial charge is typically around 5% or 6%, though some funds have a lower initial charge because of the nature of the investment. These include gilt funds, index tracker funds and money-market funds. Commission to financial advisers, usually 3%, is paid out of the initial charge.

The annual management charge is the fund manager's fee for running the portfolio. It is deducted from the fund and is therefore effectively built into the unit price. Annual charges range from 0·75% to 1·5%.

The fund has a number of other charges to pay – auditor's and trustee's fees, for instance – though they usually represent only a tiny percentage of the fund.

The fund manager can deduct these charges either from the trust's capital or from gross income. If they are deducted from income they will clearly affect the yield; if from capital, there will be a small capital loss. An income fund manager might take the view that yield is to be maintained at all costs, and deduct costs from capital.

○ *Disclosure*: Every investor who buys units should see a 'key features document', which gives information on: the investment's aims and how it works; the risks attached to buying the units; charges and expenses, and their effect on the investor's return and the amount of commission paid.

Unit trusts have always been 'transparent' in declaring charges clearly. The stricter disclosure regime introduced in 1997 makes things even clearer for investors. One effect of this may be to bring added pressure for lower charges.

○ *The annual report:* All unit trusts have to produce an annual report. Most also produce a report during the year, known as an interim report.
    The annual report should give you the following information:
○ How big is the fund?
○ Has it grown or shrunk over the year?
○ How popular has it been with unitholders?
    See 'cash received on creations' compared to 'cash paid on cancellations'.
○ What are its holdings?
    This is what your money is invested in!
○ What is its geographical/sector spread?
    The wider the spread, the lower the risk.
○ How many holdings does it have?
    The higher the number of holdings, the lower the risk.
○ How much cash is it holding?
    A big cash position suggests lack of confidence in the market – but you may want a fund that stays fully invested.
○ How many changes have been made to the portfolio?
    High turnover means high dealing costs. It could also indicate major portfolio restructuring.

Tax

UNIT TRUSTS HAVE A TAX ADVANTAGE in that the fund itself is not liable to capital gains tax. The investor is subject to both income tax on income from the fund and capital gains tax on growth in the value of the holding, see Chapter 10 for more information on tax and stock-market investment.

INCOME TAX
Income tax is payable on distributions made by the unit trust to investors. However, you will receive your distributions net of tax

UNIT TRUSTS

at the 20% rate. A tax voucher is sent with the distribution, detailing this 20% tax credit. The tax voucher should be sent to the Inland Revenue when you declare your income from the trust on your tax return.

If you are a 20% taxpayer there will be no further tax bill. If you are a non-taxpayer, you can use the voucher to reclaim the 20% tax. Higher-rate taxpayers will be liable for the difference between the 20% paid and their total bill.

Funds which invest in overseas stocks may also pay foreign income dividend distributions. These are also deemed tax paid at the 20% rate but they do not carry a tax credit, and the 20% is not recoverable.

CAPITAL GAINS TAX

Though the unit trust manager is not liable to capital gains tax within the fund, the unitholder could become liable if considerable gains accumulate within a unitholding.

Q&A

Q *Can capital gains tax on unit trusts be avoided in the same way as for shares?*

A Yes, you can 'bed and breakfast' unitholdings (see Chapter 10). Most unit trust groups and intermediaries offer special terms on this type of bargain.

Q *Can't I avoid tax altogether by investing through PEPs?*

A Yes, unit trusts are now the main type of asset held in PEP, and PEPs make up the vast majority of all unit trust sales. Some groups offer cheaper entry to some trusts through a PEP than by holding the trust without the PEP plan (see Chapter 7).

Q *If I reinvest dividends to buy more units, can I defer the income tax due?*

A No, income tax is payable for the year in which the dividend was received, whether or not you reinvest.

When to invest in unit trusts

UNIT TRUSTS are very flexible:

- ❍ They have a low minimum investment.
- ❍ They have a transparent charging structure, rather than charges that are 'built in'.
- ❍ They impose no limitations on redemption (though some trusts make an exit charge in the first few years).
- ❍ You can buy, sell or switch your holding at any time.
- ❍ There is an enormous range of unit trusts available and you can pick combinations to suit almost any investment aim or objective.

The following cases are typical examples of uses to which unit trusts might be put:

- ❍ A young married couple want to start building up savings for future uses as yet unknown. Although they have no children they envisage a possible future need for education fees or even a supplement to retirement income in the distant future. They cannot afford much, but decide on regular savings in a UK General fund, offering a mix of income and growth. They expect their savings to be long term, as they are aware that the fluctuating value of a stockmarket investment would not be suitable for, say, building up a deposit on a house which is needed in two years' time.

- ❍ An investor who has many years' experience of managing his own portfolio of shares, now worth £150,000, still uses unit trusts for some areas of investment. Even for a large investor overseas investment, especially in smaller or developing markets, is cheaper and easier through a unit trust. Unit trusts provide him with professional management in overseas markets where information is relatively hard to obtain, and they offer simplified and relatively low-cost administration.

- ❍ A student reading Latin American studies is left £1,000 by an uncle. She decides to invest it in her own area of interest, and back her hunch that Latin American markets will perform dramatically over the next year. There are a number of Latin American unit trusts which will allow you to get a piece of the action, and she chooses one whose record is good and whose investment policy suits her needs. This is obviously a high-risk strategy, and not recommended for the bulk of your savings!

○ A widow aged 66 has £30,000 from a maturing endowment policy. She has no need of further income at present, but feels she may in the future. Her family has a strong record of living to a ripe old age, so she feels it is essential to invest for growth.

She chooses a portfolio of income unit trusts with good performance records, and whose distribution dates are planned to give at least one payment in each month of the year. She decides to reinvest the income for now, but knows she can ask to have income paid out at a future date. The management group will switch her instructions free of charge.

She invests her annual limit in a PEP to reduce her tax liability, and plans to shelter more holdings in PEPs in future years.

INVESTING IN UNIT TRUSTS FOR A CHILD

Unit trusts are ideal for this purpose, especially if the aim is to build up a fund for when an infant reaches adulthood. Given a long enough term a relatively high-risk fund (such as a Far East fund) could be chosen, or investors may prefer to stick with a low-risk general fund with a good performance record.

The money can be invested for the child through a designated account, where the investor's initials are followed by those of the child – for example, Harold Jones a/c GAJ, where Harold is saving on behalf of his granddaughter, Gemma Ann Jones. The savings belong to Gemma, with Harold acting as nominee. He has the power to change the investment on her behalf.

Money invested by parents for their children counts as belonging to the parent for tax purposes. If Harold sends a cheque for Gemma to Gemma's father, he should make it clear what he is doing in a letter which can be used to make the position clear to the Revenue. A person who is under 18 cannot hold a PEP, though Harold could invest in a PEP of his own and leave the money to Gemma in his will.

Action plan

○ Decide whether unit trusts are suitable for you.

○ Assess your own investment needs and level of risk tolerance. Make sure the fund you choose fits in with this assessment.

○ Note any practical needs, like monthly income, a regular savings plan with a low minimum investment, or a group with a range of funds so your investment can be switched if necessary.

○ Check the performance record. Don't rely on the figures quoted in advertisements or fund marketing literature. Check any fund you are interested in against other funds with a similar objective, against the performance sector average and against inflation and the relevant market index. Don't worry too much about top tens. Look instead for performers which are in the top performance quartile over most periods.

○ Check the charges. You shouldn't make your decision on the basis of charges alone, because good fund performance can more than make up for a percentage point or two in charges. However, low charges combined with good performance is always a combination that's worth looking out for.

○ Consider the risk level of the fund. Many management groups rate their funds for you to give an idea of risk. Don't forget to take your other assets into account. If you have a large amount of money in the building society you can probably afford to take on some risk by making an investment in a share-based unit trust. If you are near retirement and have not got a large portfolio of savings you should stick to a safer choice like a corporate bond PEP or a balanced fund which includes some shares and some fixed interest.

○ If you are a very active private investor you may be keen to check current prices, the trust's pricing basis, and so on. An investor who intends to buy and hold for the long term should not worry too much about small, short-term price movements.

○ However, even smaller investors should have at least some awareness of major market movements. If markets have been rising for some time and are now at an all-time high, this probably wouldn't be the right moment to invest your lump sum.

○ Use our Guide to the sectors (see pages 78–79) in order to find the right unit trust category for your needs.

UNIT TRUSTS

6
Investment trusts

Perhaps what attracts you to the stockmarket is the thrill of holding shares – of feeling you own a small percentage of a working company. But you may also be worried about risk. Investment trusts were designed to give investors the best of both worlds.

Investment trusts are funds set up as companies, whose 'business' is not manufacturing or operating shops in the high street, but the buying and selling of portfolios of shares in other companies to make a profit for the investment trust shareholders.

Investment trusts are the oldest form of stockmarket investment fund for private investors. The idea for them originated in the late 19th century, to allow individuals to put money into exciting overseas ventures, such as the railways which were then spreading across the North American wild west.

As a result of this pedigree the investment trust sector has an international flavour, reflected in many of the trust's names. Perhaps the best known investment trust is Foreign & Colonial, which was established in 1868, more than 130 years ago. This trust, which in early 1997 had less than 40% of its portfolio in the UK, is the largest investment trust, reaching the FTSE 100 Index in December 1995.

By comparison, if you had bought shares in British Telecom when it was privatised in 1984, you would by September 1997 have seen your money grow by 201% – enough to convert anyone to the appeal of shareowning. But Foreign & Colonial's share price grew by 441% over the same period, which suggests investment trusts are definitely worth considering!

PERFORMANCE
Though investment trusts have not done better than the All-Share Index over all periods, they have given good returns to investors. If you had invested £100 in the average International: General Fund ten years ago, you would have ended up with more than £277 in September 1997. The best sector over the same period was North America, where £100 would have grown to £298. The

worst was Japan, which would only have given 26% growth. The UK: Income Growth sector would have produced £277 and the high-risk Venture and Development Capital sector would have given the best return at £330. Meanwhile the RPI would have inflated £100 to £154, and the FTA All-Share Index would have made it grow to almost £275.

Over a single year, the volatility of stockmarket investment was clearly in evidence: returns varied from almost 56% in the Venture and Development Capital sector to an average loss of 41% among Japan funds.

These are averages. The best performers did substantially better than the average fund. Foreign & Colonial itself, though not always a star performer, illustrates the long-term value of share fund investment.

The table shows a comparison between the Foreign & Colonial share price and an index representing the equity market as a whole. Foreign & Colonial has also chosen to compare itself not to the price of eggs, but to the cost of a pint of beer. From 1945 its 'beer index' turned £1,000 into £31,200. The investment trust's shares did better. It turned £1,000 into £956,329 – enough for almost 80,000 gallons of draught bitter!

FOREIGN & COLONIAL – THE LIPSMACKING TASTE OF SUCCESS?

Value at the end of 1996 of an investment of £100 made in December 1945

	Price of a pint of beer	Beer index	BZW Equity Index	Foreign & Colonial share price
1945	5p	£1,000	£1,000	£1,000
1960	6p	£1,200	£3,949	£9,108
1975	20p	£4,000	£9,439	£35,347
1990	110p	£22,000	£108,820	£395,275
1996	156p	£31,200	£250,170	£956,329

Source: Foreign & Colonial

How investment trusts developed

Though investment trusts were started up for private investors, they became dominated by institutional investors in the 20th century as the number of private shareholders declined. Insurance companies and pension funds started to use them as a way to harness investment expertise in what were then unfamiliar parts of the world, like Japan and the Far East.

By the 1980s, investment trusts had fallen behind in popularity. However, the industry successfully reinvented itself, partly through savings plans which allowed very small investors to buy shares by post through the trust manager. In more recent years a lot of new investment trusts have been launched, often with a complicated 'split capital' structure, and largely designed for PEP investors.

The investment trust sector generally has a good long-term performance record and because of low fund charges it remains a very cost-effective way for smaller investors to spread stock-market risk and invest in markets which would otherwise be inaccessible to them.

How investment trusts work

Investment trusts launch themselves by making a share issue in the same way as any company which seeks a stockmarket quotation. The money raised in the share issue is then invested in a portfolio of shares in the market or sector in which the fund has chosen to specialise.

Shareholders own a percentage of the fund in proportion to the number of shares they hold. The shares are bought and sold on the stockmarket like those of any other company, and the share price rises and falls accordingly. The share price will be affected by the prevailing stockmarket climate, by investors' views of the sector in which the trust invests, and by their opinion of the management company's expertise.

The investment trust share price may not exactly reflect the current value of the underlying investment portfolio. It may be lower or higher than the assets in the fund are actually worth. If the share price is lower than the net asset value per share, the trust is said to be at a discount. If it is higher, the trust is at a premium.

Unlike unit trusts, investment trusts cannot constantly issue and cancel shares. They are therefore known as closed-end funds.

They can make new share issues from time to time if they want to raise extra money, and they can issue a number of different types of share.

They can also borrow in order to increase the money available to invest. This leads to an effect in the portfolio known as 'gearing', which can be used to enhance performance quite dramatically, though it also means increased risk for the investor.

Like any class of shareholder, investment trust shareholders may get capital growth through a rise in the share price of their holding (or a loss if the fund does badly and the share price falls). They will also get income, as with shares in trading companies, usually through a half-yearly dividend, unless the trust invests in holdings which have a low or nil yield.

There is no specified investment term with investment trusts – you can buy and sell them at any time, just like a quoted share. However, like any stockmarket investment, they should only be entered into for the long term. There is also no formal minimum investment, although investment trusts carry stockbrokers' dealing costs, which effectively means there is a minimum viable investment of, say, £1,000 or so if you buy through a stockbroker.

Investment trust savings plans save the formality of dealing through a stockbroker and allow people to invest very small sums. In practice, this is how most private investors buy investment trust shares.

Q&A

Q Do investment trusts have a trust structure in the legal sense?
A No. One thing investment trusts are not is trusts! Investment trusts have a corporate structure just like any high-street company, and are properly called 'investment trust companies', though for brevity they are often known as 'trusts'.

Q Do investment trusts have a maturity date?
A No, ordinary investment trusts have no predetermined winding up date, though the special type known as split capital trusts do. They are explained in more detail later in this chapter.

WHERE CAN YOU INVEST?

There are currently 19 investment sectors listed by the Association of Investment Trust Companies (AITC) (see 'Guide to the invest-

Independent financial adviser and *Moneywise* Ask the Professionals panellist Kean Seager says:

"Investment trusts offer an extremely wide range of investment options from low risk to high risk, from domestic to all international markets in the world."

ment trust sectors' on pages 108 and 109). As the box shows, there are plenty of funds in the more general categories, such as International: Capital Growth or UK Income Growth, which also offer a spread of investment and therefore a wider spread of risk. Chapter 5 discusses the risk levels of different types of fund in more detail.

But higher risk specialist funds like smaller companies and venture capital are also thriving. Investment trusts are a natural vehicle for this type of holding because the funds are closed-end. In other words, the fund manager does not have buying or selling decisions forced on him or her by the demand, or lack of demand, for shares. The fund manager does not have to sell investments in order to pay back investors, as a unit trust manager might if there was a run of redemptions on his or her fund.

This feature of investment trusts makes them particularly suitable for illiquid investments (that is, investments which are not always easy to sell in a hurry) like unquoted companies. Investors should remember that the level of risk attached to investment trusts can vary a lot between different types of fund – more so than with unit trusts. You should not invest a large proportion of your capital in an investment trust which holds a high percentage of speculative start-ups.

TRADING AT A DISCOUNT

In recent times most investment trusts have tended to trade at a discount. That is, the share price was lower than the value of net assets attributable to each share. The discount is expressed as a percentage of the net asset value. So, if the net asset value is 100p, a discount of 15% would give a share price of 85p. The investor who buys at that price is effectively buying shares worth 100p for 15% off.

If the share price moves to 105p, but the net asset value stays the same, the trust is said to be at a 5% premium. This would usually be shown as +5. In this case, the investor is paying more for the portfolio of shares than they are actually worth on the market. Why would an investor do that? Because he or she regards the

Guide to the investment trust sectors

(The number of trusts in each sector at 1.9.97 is shown in brackets)

KEY

- £ = low/no yield
- ££ = moderate yields
- £££ = high yields
- $/! = overseas currency risk

- ! = low risk
- !! = moderate risk
- !!! = high risk
- !!!! = very high risk

- I = good for income investors
- G = good for growth investors

INTERNATIONAL: GENERAL (15)

Investment trusts which invest in a spread of international markets, with less than 80% of assets in any one area.
££ !! G $/!

INTERNATIONAL: INCOME GROWTH (5)

As for International: General trusts, but with an investment emphasis on growth of income.
£££ !! I $/!

INTERNATIONAL: CAPITAL GROWTH (28)

As for International: General trusts, but with an investment emphasis on achieving capital growth.
£ !! G $/!

UK: GENERAL (17)

Investment trusts which have at least 80% of their assets in UK companies.
£ !! G

UK: INCOME GROWTH (21)

Trusts with at least 80% of assets in the UK, and an emphasis on income growth.
££ !! I G

UK: CAPITAL GROWTH (15)

Trusts with at least 80% in the UK and an emphasis on capital growth.
£ !! G

HIGH INCOME (13)

Trusts with at least 80% invested in equities and convertibles, aiming to achieve a yield of at least 125% that of the FT-A All-Share Index.
£££ ! I

NORTH AMERICA (10)

Trusts with at least 80% of assets in North America.
£ !!! G $/!

FAR EAST, EXCLUDING JAPAN (25)

Trusts with at least 80% of assets in Far Eastern markets, but with no holdings in the Japanese market. Trusts may invest in a number of markets or a single market.
£ !!! G $/!

FAR EAST, INCLUDING JAPAN (6)

Trusts with at least 80% of assets in the Far East, including a Japanese content of less than 80% of the total.
£ !!! G $/!

JAPAN (14)

Trusts with at least 80% of assets in the Japanese market.
£ !!! G

PROPERTY (4)

Trusts with at least 80% in shares in the property sector of the stockmarket. These are mostly UK funds, but may also be international.
£ !!! G

CONTINENTAL EUROPE (20)

Trusts with at least 80% of assets in Continental Europe. Trusts may invest in a number of markets or in a single market.
£ !!! G $/!

PAN EUROPE (3)

Trusts with at least 80% of assets in Europe, including the UK, but with at least 40% in Continental Europe.
£ !!! G $/!

COMMODITY & ENERGY (3)

Trusts with at least 80% in the shares of commodity and energy companies.
£ !!!! G

EMERGING MARKETS (30)

Trusts with at least 80% in emerging markets. Trusts may invest in a range of markets or a single market.
£ !!!! G $/!

CLOSED-END FUNDS (6)

Trusts which invest at least 80% in other closed-end funds.
££ !! G

SMALLER COMPANIES (43)

Trusts with at least 50% of the value of the portfolio in smaller- or medium-sized companies.
£ !!! G

VENTURE & DEVELOPMENT CAPITAL (29)

Trusts which invest in new ventures or new developments in existing companies. A significant proportion of assets may be in the shares of unquoted companies.
£ !!!! G

fund as likely to show a good investment return – enough to make it worth his or her while paying over the odds.

The level of discount or premium may be related to the fund category. For instance, in September 1997 investors were more cautious about some overseas sectors than others. Both North American and Far Eastern trusts had an average discount (size-weighted) of 10%. The average for Continental European funds was only 6%. Meanwhile, some of the large, well-known International: General funds were at discounts of up to 18% – a bargain for the long-term investor.

Discounts show general movement from time to time. Towards the end of the 1980s discounts narrowed (that is, got smaller) over the whole investment trust sector. Specialist trusts tend to show the most exaggerated discount movements because they offer expertise which may be attractive to institutional investors, but in areas which may go in and out of fashion.

Trusts with a general investment objective tend to have fairly wide discounts and do not often go to a premium, because they are of relatively little interest to the institutions. But discounts can move from time to time on any fund.

The discount can benefit the investor in two ways:

○ By buying shares for less then their inherent worth, you are harnessing extra assets to generate a return. Your 85p is buying 100p worth of assets which may produce capital growth as well as dividends. It is a bit like putting 85p into an interest-paying account, but getting interest on 100p.

○ The discount could work to your advantage when you buy and sell. Suppose you buy at 85p, when the net asset value is 100p. You hold your shares for a time, then sell when the discount is only 5%. In addition to the growth on your shares, you have effectively gained a 10% boost to your return.

There is another problem for investment trusts that is linked to the discount. Like any other company an investment trust can fall victim to a takeover. If the trust is trading at

Independent financial adviser and *Moneywise* Ask the Professionals panellist Kean Seager says:

"Discounts give you a greater opportunity to make money, but entail more risk because share values fluctuate more than unit trusts. Buying investment trusts at a premium is usually not a good idea because you're buying an expensively valued asset."

a big discount it will be attractive to a potential predator, who could buy it at its market value and sell off the assets, making a gain on the deal. If this happens, shareholders will not lose out in cash terms. They should get an enhanced cash value for their shares, which they will have to re-invest elsewhere. This is one reason why investment trusts are anxious to recruit private investors as shareholders. Small investors may be less keen to see their investment trust disappear, whereas the institutional investors who hold the majority of shares in many trusts are unlikely to be so loyal.

Q&A

Q I am nervous of investing in investment trusts because I know the discount changes all the time. Should I just avoid them?

A No. Small investors, who, in any case, ought to be investing for the long term, do not need to worry about such discount changes. If you hold your shares for a number of years, growth in the fund is likely to outweigh any adverse effect from changes in the discount.

Q When I am choosing an investment trust, is the best advice just to go for the biggest discount?

A No. A very big discount, which is out of line with that of other trusts in the same category may mean that there is some specific reason for the trust's share price to be marked down. If anything, you should avoid a trust in these circumstances. The ideal strategy is to choose a fund where the discount is undeservedly large, and the market is likely to revalue the fund in the future, but this calls for expert knowledge. Most private investors should not worry about discounts, though they should perhaps avoid investing a large lump sum when the trust is at a premium.

Q I am an investment trust regular saver, buying shares through a savings plan each month. What if the trust I have chosen goes to a premium?

A It is as well to monitor your investment, but don't worry if the trust goes to a premium temporarily. If you save over several years, the times when it is at a discount will probably compensate.

Investment trust gearing: when all goes well

A new investment trust is launched, with the following capital structure:

	£
£85m ordinary shares (85m shares at £1)	85,000,000
£15m debenture (loan) stock	15,000,000
Initial value of portfolio	**100,000,000**
Net asset value per ordinary share = £1	
After five years the trust's portfolio has increased in value by 100%:	
Value of portfolio	200,000,000
Less value of debenture	15,000,000
	185,000,000

Net asset value per ordinary share = £2·18
(£185m divided by 85m)

Where the fund has increased in value by 100%, the share price has gone up by 118%.

GEARING

Apart from the discount, the other unfamiliar and technical aspect of investment trusts is gearing. We have already seen the term gearing used in connection with reading a company's report and accounts. In investment trust terms, gearing means boosting performance by borrowing.

It works like this. The trust makes an issue of loan stock. The issue will usually be taken up by institutions, who will receive a fixed rate of interest. The money raised from the issue is invested to enhance the fund. Hopefully, it will increase both the capital and income growth return to the investor.

The secret of gearing is that if the fund is invested successfully, the benefit to the investor will be much greater than the actual growth in the portfolio. The bad news is that the effect works in

Investment trust gearing: when things go wrong

The share price of the fund now falls by 30%

	£
Value of portfolio (£200m less 30%)	140,000,000
Less value of debenture	15,000,000
	125,000,000

Net asset value per ordinary share = £1·47 (£125m divided by 85m)

Where the fund has decreased in value by 30%, the share price has gone down by 33%.

reverse if the fund makes a loss. This particular magic act can only be explained by using an example.

The box on page 112 shows a new investment trust with 85 million £1 shares and £15 million in loan stock. Over five years the value of the fund doubles, but the share price more than doubles: it is up by 118%.

If we then suppose that the share price falls by 30%, the box above shows that the effect of gearing is to reduce the share price by 33%. The reason gearing works in this way is because it represents a fixed element of the portfolio. The loan income contributes to the full growth of the portfolio, but as the total portfolio value increases the gearing represents a smaller and smaller liability.

Gearing will also affect income (see box on page 114). The fund manager has to choose a moment when interest rates are reasonably low in order to make gearing viable. The loan stock has to be issued at a better rate than comparable gilts, to make it attractive to the buying institutions. Though gearing increases losses in the investment trust when markets fall, it can easily be 'undone' by selling shares and moving into cash and gilts. If a trust is 20% geared (which would be considered high) but holds 5% in cash, it is effectively only 15% geared.

As far as the investor is concerned, gearing increases the risk of an investment trust, but will also increase the potential rewards.

Investment trust gearing: income boost

The fund portfolio is invested to yield 4%

First year	£
Income from portfolio (4% x £100,000,000)	4,000,000
Less debenture interest (8% x £15,000,000)	1,200,000
Gross income attributable to 85m ordinary shares	**2,800,000**
Dividend per share (£2,800,000 divided by 85m)	3·29p
Five years later	
Income from portfolio (4% x £200,000,000)	8,000,000
Less debenture interest (8% x £15,000,000)	1,200,000
Gross income attributable to 85m ordinary shares	**6,800,000**
Dividend per share (£6,800,000 divided by 85m)	8p

Where the fund has increased in value by 100%, the dividend has gone up by more than 140%.

Some experts say that gearing, one of the principal features that sets investment trusts aside from other investment funds, is under-used by trust managers.

SPLIT CAPITAL INVESTMENT TRUSTS

If discounts and gearing are not technical enough for you, you might want to get to grips with split capital investment trusts or 'splits'. These are trusts with two or more types of share, each of which carries different benefits and levels of risk. Some offer good returns for little risk. Others can have surprisingly high risks attached.

Many split capital trusts have been launched in the last ten years and some are very complicated, with up to six different classes of share. If you are considering investing in splits it is important to get advice from a specialist.

An important feature of split capital trusts is the fact that they have a fixed winding-up date, when the portfolio proceeds are split among the different classes of shareholder, according to entitlement.

Some shares rank before others in the pecking order on redemption, and this clearly has a bearing on how risky they are. A preference share which has first call on the trust's assets will be less risky than a capital share which has to wait until last for its payout.

The original idea of split capital trusts was to provide a more tax-effective form of investment. Trusts had capital shares, which received all the capital growth on the portfolio, and income shares which got all the income. The capital shares would not create a liability to income tax – useful for the higher-rate taxpayer – and the income shares would offer enhanced yield – a boon to the income seeker.

The effect was that someone who had, say, invested £1,000 in capital shares, for example, would get the growth on £2,000, and the income investor putting in £1,000 would get the income on £2,000. In other words, split capital trusts create another type of gearing.

In the last few years more classes of share have been introduced into split capital trusts, each offering a slightly different type of return.

○ *Capital shares*: In newer split capital trusts capital shares are last in the pecking order for payment when the trust is wound up. In a complex trust structure there may be as many as five other classes of share ahead of them in the queue for payment on wind-up. They can therefore be quite risky.
○ *Income shares*: There are a number of different variants on the income share theme. Some income shares have a capital

entitlement on redemption, but are linked to zero dividend preference shares (see below), which rank ahead of them in the final payout. Though the capital entitlement enhances the possible return, the need to repay the zeros first increases the risk. Another type of income share is the annuity share, which pays a very high yield, but has little or no value upon redemption.

O *Stepped preference shares*: These have a predetermined rate of return of both capital and income, which increases year on year. They are first in line to receive their entitlement when the trust is wound up. They are relatively low risk, and offer a predictable and growing return, but yields may be low compared to those of income shares.

O *Zero dividend preference shares*: 'Zeros' pay no income, but have a fixed redemption price, offering a built-in capital return. They are designed to be tax-effective, since they do not create an income liability. But the redemption price is not guaranteed, and since there may be other classes of share ahead of the zeros in the queue, it should not be assumed that all zeros are safe.

That said, there are zeros which offer a low-risk return. The measure is the hurdle rate – the rate by which the fund portfolio must grow in each remaining year of its life if the shares are to be paid off in full.

A zero with a hurdle rate of 7%, and three years in which to wind up, would be in danger of not being redeemed in full. However, a zero with a negative hurdle rate is very safe – this means that the fund value will have to fall each year until redemption before the zeros are in any danger. Hurdle rates are used for all types of share in which there is a fixed redemption value.

INVESTMENT TRUST WARRANTS

Many investment trusts have warrants in issue (see Chapter 4). They may be given free if you buy shares in a newly launched investment trust. Warrants attached to investment trust shares work in exactly the same way as warrants in the wider market. Conventional investment trust warrants subscribe into ordinary shares. Warrants attached to split capital trusts subscribe into one or two specific classes of share.

Questions to ask before investing in split capital trust shares

1 What are the shares' entitlement on redemption?

2 How likely are they to see this level of return?

3 How many years are left before the trust is wound up?

4 What is the shares' position in the pecking order?

5 What is the hurdle rate?

6 What will be the effect of this investment for tax purposes?

7 What is the yield during the life of the investment?

8 What will the redemption yield be at different growth rates?

9 What capital return can I expect?

When warrants are exercised they 'dilute' the trust's net asset value per share, because the exercise price of the warrant will usually be lower than the net asset value. Existing assets together with exercise money from warrants are combined, and are spread across a higher number of shares than before. The result is a reduction in net asset value for all shareholders. Investment trusts which have warrants publish net asset values in both undiluted and diluted forms.

How to buy

There are two ways to buy investment trusts:

○ *Through a stockbroker*: Smaller investors will find it too cumbersome to approach a stockbroker just for a small purchase of investment trust shares. Larger investors may find it useful to approach a stockbroker who specialises in investment trusts. Some stockbrokers offer an investment trust management service, where they will run a portfolio of investment trusts on your behalf. If you buy through a stockbroker you will have to pay normal brokerage rates on purchases and sales (see Chapter 9).

Similarities and differences between unit and investment trusts

SIMILARITIES

○ Both investment trusts and unit trusts pool investors' money together and invest it.

○ Both types of fund are able to invest in the same types of companies all over the world.

○ You can hold unit trusts and investment trusts in a Personal Equity Plan.

○ Both types of fund are managed by professional fund managers.

DIFFERENCES

○ Investors in a unit trust receive units, investors in investment trusts receive shares.

○ With an investment trust the share price is not directly related to the value underlying investments.

○ An investment trust can borrow money to boost its investments.

○ Investment trusts are closed-ended – in otherwords the number of shares in issue is fixed. Unit trusts are open-ended – so new units can be issued on demand, and cancelled when investors cash in.

○ *Through a savings scheme* Much cheaper and more convenient than dealing through a stockbroker, savings schemes allow you to buy investment trust shares by post through the investment trust manager. The manager does not sell you the shares in person. Like all shares, they can only be bought and sold through the stockmarket itself. However, he or she will bundle together all savings scheme dealings and deal at very favourable rates through a broker. Some schemes charge nothing at all for purchases, and only a nominal percentage for sales.

Savings schemes are particularly good for small savers. A number will still accept as little as £25 a month or a lump sum of £250. Many investment trusts can also be held through a PEP, and a number of these plans also have very low charges, as well as being tax free.

Q&A

Q Don't investment trusts have fund charges?

A Yes, they do. The fund manager levies an annual charge. Older investment trusts often have very low charges – typically below 0·5%. Newer trusts may have higher annual charges, approaching those of unit trusts. Investment trusts do not have initial charges like unit trusts, but you will have to pay dealing costs when you buy and sell, depending on how you deal.

Action plan

1 Look again at the flowchart in Chapter 1 (page 21) to decide whether you should invest in funds rather than directly in shares.

2 Look also at the risk chart in Chapter 1 (page 18) to see where your needs are on the risk spectrum.

3 If you are a smaller investor needing a low risk home for your money, you should look at general trusts with an income objective (International: General or UK: Income Growth, for example). The Association of Investment Trust Companies offers a good deal of free information, including performance figures, to help you choose.

4 Savings schemes offered by the fund managers are cheap and simple, though you need to make your own decision on which fund to invest in. Regular savers will benefit from pound cost averaging (see Chapter 5).

5 If you want advice on a whole portfolio of investments, on specialist funds or on more complicated areas like split capital trusts or warrants, seek advice. Make sure the person you speak to has some expertise in investment trusts (many advisers may not).

6 Monitor your investment, but don't worry too much in the short term about changes in the discount.

7 Personal equity plans

For most smaller investors who want to put money into the stockmarket, a Personal Equity Plan (PEP) is probably the most obvious vehicle to choose as it gives the advantage of tax-free stockmarket returns. Because of this benefit a PEP will out-perform an identical investment plan which is not 'PEPed'.

The plan can be made up of any of a variety of assets: pooled funds like unit trusts or investment trusts, shares, and even some cash and fixed-interest investments. As this book was going to press, it was possible for the private investor to shelter a total of £9,000 a year from tax within a PEP.

PEPs first appeared in January 1987. They were designed to attract individual investors into the stockmarket, and so increase the percentage of shareholdings in private hands. The emphasis initially was on direct shareholdings, and the maximum you could save was £2,400 a year. This maximum was quickly increased. If you had put the full allowance into a PEP each year from the start, by the tax year 1997/98 you would have invested £79,200. A married couple could have put in this amount each, giving a sizeable nest egg for their retirement.

With a successful choice of investments, it is quite possible that your holding might have doubled in value. Rumour has it that there is a canny investor out there with a strong stomach for risks who has built up a £1m PEP account!

It was also recognised as time went on that funds like unit trusts and investment trusts made more sense for the smaller investor than directly held shares. Unit trusts and investment trusts accounted for almost two-thirds of all PEP investments by 1995.

When PEPs began the aim was to draw investment into the UK stockmarket. Investment, therefore, was to be almost exclusively in the UK, and in equities only: no fixed interest. From 1992 the PEP geographical limit was widened to the whole of the European

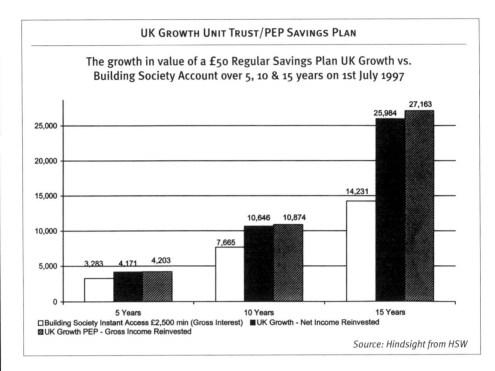

UK GROWTH UNIT TRUST/PEP SAVINGS PLAN

The growth in value of a £50 Regular Savings Plan UK Growth vs.
Building Society Account over 5, 10 & 15 years on 1st July 1997

□ Building Society Instant Access £2,500 min (Gross Interest) ■ UK Growth - Net Income Reinvested
▨ UK Growth PEP - Gross Income Reinvested

Source: Hindsight from HSW

Union. From 1995 investors could also put money into corporate bonds (see Chapter 8). This made PEPs more useful to those wanting high income and a shelter from equity market risk.

But the end of the PEP era is in sight. In his July 1997 Budget, the Chancellor of the Exchequer announced that PEPs would be replaced by Individual Savings Accounts (ISAs) in 1999. As this book was going to press there were few details on how ISAs would work, or what the tax benefits and investment limits would be, but it is clear that savings with a tax incentive will continue into the new millennium.

Tax expert and *Moneywise* Ask the Professionals panellist Janet Adam says:

"Despite the changes on the horizon, PEPs continue to provide tax advantages, particularly to higher-rate taxpayers who already use up their capital gains tax allowance."

HOW THE TAX BREAKS HELP

The success or otherwise of a PEP will depend primarily on the performance of the assets it contains. Charges will also play a part. But its ultimate usefulness to you will depend on whether it

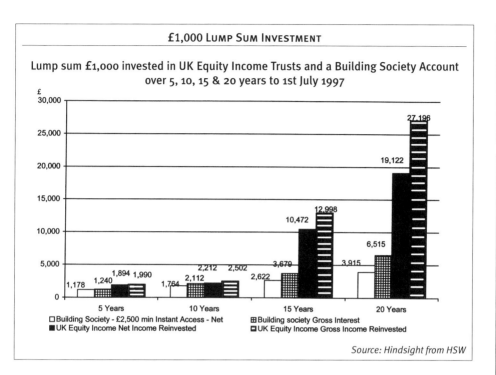

£1,000 Lump Sum Investment

Lump sum £1,000 invested in UK Equity Income Trusts and a Building Society Account over 5, 10, 15 & 20 years to 1st July 1997

Legend:
- ☐ Building Society - £2,500 min Instant Access - Net
- ⊞ Building society Gross Interest
- ■ UK Equity Income Net Income Reinvested
- ◨ UK Equity Income Gross Income Reinvested

Source: Hindsight from HSW

fits your investment requirements and in particular on whether you can leave the plan untouched for a long time.

A PEP plan is as good as the shares or funds in which it is invested. The graph on page 122 shows a notional comparison between an average UK growth unit trust, the same fund held in a PEP, and a building society instant access account. The difference in return between the equity investments and the building society is substantial after only five years. After 15 years the PEP investor would have made almost twice as much as the building society account holder. This reiterates the point about the benefits of long-term stockmarket investment, as illustrated in Chapter 1.

The difference between the unit trust and the unit trust PEP reflects the PEP's tax advantage. Because the fund chosen is a growth fund, offering a low or nil yield, the tax saving is not great. A substantial difference is only seen after 15 years.

The graph above makes a similar comparison between UK income funds and the building society. Here the PEP advantage is seen sooner and more markedly, reflecting the higher income tax saving made on the equity income fund.

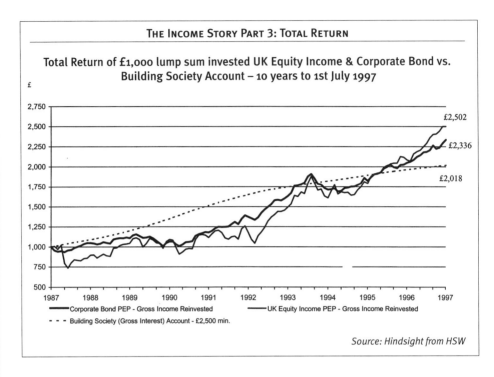

Total Return of £1,000 lump sum invested UK Equity Income & Corporate Bond vs. Building Society Account – 10 years to 1st July 1997

£2,502
£2,336
£2,018

Corporate Bond PEP - Gross Income Reinvested
UK Equity Income PEP - Gross Income Reinvested
- - - Building Society (Gross Interest) Account - £2,500 min.

Source: Hindsight from HSW

Finally, the graph above shows how an equity income PEP and a corporate bond PEP outpaced a building society account (shown without deduction of tax). From this graph it is easy to see how, in the early years, the PEP produced a poorer return than the building society, and was much more volatile. Longer term, however, both corporate bonds and equity income showed better gains than the building society, which was beaten by 16% and 24% respectively.

PEP RULES

○ *Who can hold a PEP?* Anyone who is over 18 and resident in the UK. PEPs cannot be held in joint names, but a husband and wife can each have a full PEP allowance.

○ *Is there more than one type of PEP?* There are two main types: general PEPs allow you to invest in the full range of assets and in as many holdings as your plan will permit. Single company PEPs allow you to hold shares in one company at a time. You cannot hold unit trusts or investment trusts in a single company PEP.

○ *How much can you invest?* The general PEP allowance is £6,000 for each tax year. The single company PEP allowance is £3,000.

○ *What is the minimum investment?* The minimum you can invest will depend on the plan manager. Some plans will only accept a fairly large lump sum investment – say £1,000-plus. Others will accept investment by regular monthly contributions of as little as £30–£50.

○ *Who will set up a PEP for you?* You can't set up your own PEP. It has to be set up by an authorised plan manager, who could be a fund manager, a stockbroker or an investment adviser.

○ *What are the benefits?* All gains from your PEP are free of income tax and capital gains tax. You do not need to declare your PEP on your tax return.

○ *How many plans can you have?* You can have one general PEP and one single company PEP each year – you are not allowed to spread your general PEP allowance across two plans with two different managers. Though your general PEP can be held with a different manager from your single company PEP. If you want to continue investing after the first year you can continue with the same manager or switch to a different manager.

○ *Which assets can be included?* Shares, unit trusts, investment trusts and certain types of corporate fixed-interest bond are all permitted investments for PEPs. Different PEP plans may use a single class of asset or different combinations of permitted assets.

○ *Can you hold anything else at all?* Yes. You can invest up to £1,500 each year in unit trusts or investment trusts which do not invest in permitted assets. An example might be a fund investing in an Asian market. Such funds are called 'non-qualifying' funds. The rest of the investment in your PEP must be in 'qualifying funds', which themselves have to hold at least 50% of their portfolio in permitted PEP investments. Not all PEPs will offer you the choice of non-qualifying investments.

○ *Can you keep your money in cash?* Yes, if your chosen plan allows it you can hold some money in cash within your PEP, but only as a temporary measure prior to investing in the market. There are no precise rules as to how much cash you can hold, and for how long, but the Inland Revenue could take steps to remove your tax benefits if it did not feel you were genuinely intending to invest.

○ *Do PEPs have a fixed maturity date?* No. You can sell your PEP holding at any time. Some fund PEPs have an exit charge if you sell within the first five years. Others may make a charge

125

on withdrawals. This means your money is not tied up – but early redemption is not advisable, because a PEP, like any stockmarket investment, should be regarded as a long-term holding.

○ *Can I take income from a PEP?* Yes, if you hold shares or funds which pay a dividend the PEP rules allow you either to take an income or reinvest the money to buy more shares or units. However, not all plans allow both options. Some may reinvest your income automatically. A plan which has been specially set up to pay an income may not offer the reinvestment option. Income is usually paid half yearly, though some plans pay quarterly and a few monthly.

Q&A

Q What about charges?

A PEP charges vary a lot, and it is worth checking to see that the costs on your chosen plan are not over the odds. We look at this in more detail in 'Charges', on page 132.

Q Does the £6,000 limit include charges?

A The rules allow you to invest up to the limit plus charges, but not all plan managers allow this.

Q Can I take out a PEP on behalf of my baby grandson?

A No. Only someone over 18 can take out a PEP. The only thing you can do is take out your own PEP and leave it to your grandson in your will.

Q What if I am not satisfied with my PEP's performance?

A You can transfer your PEP to another manager, but you should think carefully before doing so, as the costs outweigh the benefits. You can lose your PEP benefits altogether if you don't follow the correct procedure (see page 135).

Q Are there any other circumstances in which you can lose your PEP benefits?

A If you sell the whole of one year's PEP investment, you have lost your benefits for that year – you can't reinvest. There are no rules for carrying forward unused PEP allowances as there are for personal pensions, so if you don't invest the maximum in one tax year you have lost the chance to top up your plan to the limit. If you open two plans of the same type in one year your plan could be voided by the Inland Revenue – you have to give your national insurance number on the application form as a check.

Q What happens to my PEP if I die?
A The PEP benefits are cut off from the date of your death. The fund forms part of your estate like any other investment, and is taxable in the hands of your heirs.

Types of PEP

ALTHOUGH THERE ARE basically only two types of PEP, there are several hundred different plans on the market which are available from two hundred or more plan managers.

PEPs fall into a large number of different categories, depending mainly on:
○ whether they are general or single company PEPs.
○ whether you choose your own investments or the manager does it for you.
○ the types of asset in which the plan invests.

The PEP family tree (see page 128) summarises the types of PEP available. At its simplest a PEP might offer investment in a single unit trust. At its most complex it might combine shares, unit trusts and investment trusts with a range of investment objectives, part of the portfolio being chosen by the investor and part of it by the manager.

Here are some of the main varieties of PEP to consider:
○ *Unit trust, investment trust or share PEPs*: A general PEP can hold any of these assets. Some PEPs hold only one sort, but all combinations can be found.
○ *Corporate bond PEPs (CBPs)*: Corporate bonds are not usually mixed with other assets in PEPs, so they form a category on their own. Corporate bond PEPs were designed to allow fixed-interest investment for PEP investors – that is, higher yields than is possible with equities and greater security of capital.

127

The PEP family tree

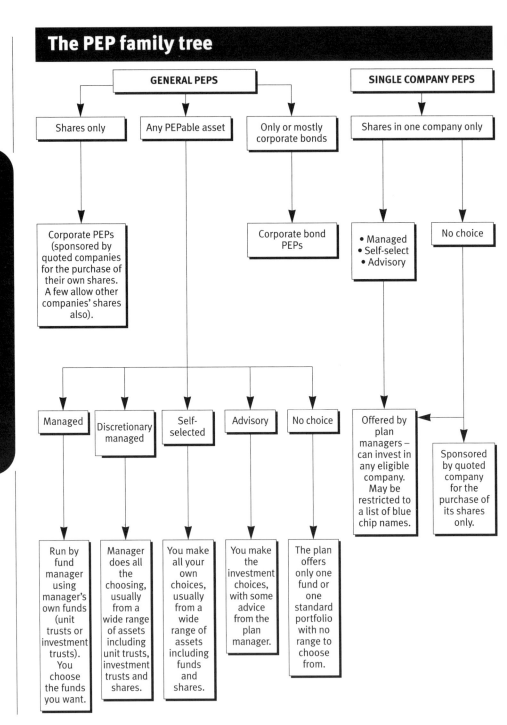

GENERAL PEPS

- Shares only
- Any PEPable asset
- Only or mostly corporate bonds

SINGLE COMPANY PEPS

- Shares in one company only

Corporate PEPs (sponsored by quoted companies for the purchase of their own shares. A few allow other companies' shares also).

Corporate bond PEPs

- Managed
- Self-select
- Advisory

No choice

Managed

Discretionary managed

Self-selected

Advisory

No choice

Offered by plan managers – can invest in any eligible company. May be restricted to a list of blue chip names.

Sponsored by quoted company for the purchase of its shares only.

Run by fund manager using manager's own funds (unit trusts or investment trusts). You choose the funds you want.

Manager does all the choosing, usually from a wide range of assets including unit trusts, investment trusts and shares.

You make all your own choices, usually from a wide range of assets including funds and shares.

You make the investment choices, with some advice from the plan manager.

The plan offers only one fund or one standard portfolio with no range to choose from.

128

CBPs were seen as a halfway house between building societies and the equity market.

Remember that with a corporate bond fund neither the capital value nor the yield is guaranteed. Although yields are normally higher than on equity funds, CBPs are not a good vehicle for providing long-term growth of either capital or income.

○ *Managed, self-select, advisory, no choice*: With a managed fund PEP you usually make the overall choice of funds yourself from the fund manager's own range. If the PEP is under 'manager's discretion' the PEP manager will do all the choosing, from a specified range of assets across the whole market. Self-select means you make all the choices yourself, from one or more holdings.

Advisory PEPs are fewer in number. In this case, the fund manager will give you advice on your choice of investments. No choice PEPs offer only one holding – a single unit trust, for instance. They are self-select in the sense that you choose the PEP yourself, but within the plan itself there is only one asset on offer.

○ *Single company PEPs (SCPs)*: These have a £3,000 a year limit and must hold one company's shares only, though different companies can be chosen in different years. SCPs may be self-select. You can also sell your original choice and buy shares in a different company – as long as you only hold one company's shares at a time.

Your plan manager may choose a company for you; in this case you just go along with the plan choice, which will usually change from one year to the next. There may be separate growth and income options. Some groups offer a general PEP + SCP package so you can use up the full £9,000 allowance in one go.

Many quoted companies offer SCPs for dealing in their own shares, and these are usually very cheap. They have the disadvantage that if you sell the shares you have lost the PEP allowance for that year. SCPs are, of course, more risky than general PEPs because your investment is tied to the share price of only one company, and they are not usually suitable for smaller general investors.

Company SCPs may appeal to employees who want PEP tax benefits on shareholdings which they have bought through an employee share savings scheme. This is feasible for someone who intends to stay with the company for a long time, and the low charges will make it very attractive, though it does mean building up a large shareholding in a single company without the flexibility to achieve a wider spread of investments.

○ *Corporate PEPs*: These are general PEPs operated by quoted companies to permit holdings in their own shares up to the annual £6,000 limit. Like company SCPs, they can be very cheap. Some now offer a choice of other shares or funds in addition to the shares of the company itself, which makes them much more flexible than SCPs.

WHICH PEP SHOULD YOU CHOOSE?

There are a number of reasons for investing in PEPs, and a number of investment strategies you could use.

Q&A

Q *How many holdings should I have in my PEP?*

A This will depend on size. With £3,000 or less you should stick to one or two holdings at most. With £6,000 you could choose a maximum of four different investments, though if you are putting your money into a fund with a spread of holdings, one investment may still be enough.

As your portfolio gets bigger, so should the unit size of your investments. For a portfolio of £20,000 to £30,000, invest in units of £4,000 to £5,000. Otherwise, you will end up with lots and lots of small holdings, which will be hard to keep track of.

Q *Can PEPs really be an alternative to pensions?*

A PEPs should not be seen as an alternative to pensions, but they can be used to supplement pension provision. They do not have tax relief on contributions as pensions do, but they will eventually offer a tax-free income. You can get at your PEP savings in the interim, whereas money in a pension is locked away until retirement – but this may be a bad thing if you find you are continually tempted to draw on the fund.

Q *Can I change my original PEP investment choice?*

A Yes, provided there are other investments on offer within the PEP, and it is either managed or self-select, you can ask the plan manager to sell one investment and buy another. Check on the charges involved, and don't be tempted to chop and change too often.

Which PEP is for you?

Do you expect to invest small amounts (less than £3,000 lump sum or £100 per month regular savings)?

Do you expect to invest all or nearly all the full PEP allowance for several years?

Do you already have an investment spread, including some stockmarket investments?

No   **Yes**

Do you want to make your own investment choices?

Do you prefer to leave the choice to a professional?

Stick to unit trust or investment trust PEPs, at least initially.

Are you investing new money?

Are you transferring existing investments into a PEP?

Get a financial adviser to help with your choice of funds.

Look for low-cost 'bed & PEP' arrangements.

Stick to unit trust or investment trust PEPs. Do some research by reading the press and choose management groups with well spread funds and a good name for performance.

Do you prefer to make your own investment choices?

Do you prefer to leave it to the professionals?

Do you prefer to make your own investment choices?

Do you need income?

Do you need
• Growth
• A balance between income and growth?

Choose a unit trust or investment trust PEP with a wide range of funds OR a self select PEP with a wide range of assets.

Ask an adviser to recommend a managed PEP or choose a discretionary managed plan (see text).

Choose a low-cost self select PEP which includes a wide range of assets, including some non-qualifying funds.

Look at corporate bond PEPs, or UK equity income funds if immediate high yield is not a priority.

Choose a combination of investment trusts with an international spread, and UK equity income and index tracker funds. Look for strong historic performance.

PERSONAL EQUITY PLANS

131

Examples

PENSION TOP-UP

A marketing manager aged 55 has a good corporate pension, and has made the maximum contribution to his company's additional voluntary contributions (AVCs) scheme. His wife does not work and therefore is not eligible for a personal pension. The couple decide to use their spare cash to fund PEPs in each of their names. They aim to build up a fund which can be drawn on in later years, either for special needs of their grown-up children, or as a tax-free boost to their retirement income.

MORTGAGE SUPPORT

A couple in their mid-30s are buying a new house – their first family home. Their lender suggests a 25-year interest only mortgage backed by an endowment policy. They do not like the idea of endowments, having read adverse comments in the press about hidden costs which can affect performance. They have a PEP plan already, and decide to increase payments into it and use it to support their mortgage. The idea of a tax-free fund is attractive, the PEP has no front-end charges, and since it has no fixed term they will be able to pay off their mortgage early if fund performance is good.

INCOME BOOST

A retired couple, both aged 70, have been left £35,000 by an elderly relative. They are basic-rate taxpayers, and any increase in their income will mean a particularly high tax penalty due to loss of age allowance. Nevertheless, they could do with an income boost.

Because of their age, growth is not a major consideration, though they would like to preserve their capital in order to pass it on to their children. They discover that they can transfer the whole sum into PEPs by investing half just before and half after the tax year end, using both PEP allowances.

They are advised to put 60% into corporate bond funds and 40% into UK equity income funds and shares. With yields of 7% on the bonds and 4.5% on the equity portfolio they get a tax-free income injection of around £2,000 a year. Their capital should be preserved and there is some possibility of growth over a number of years.

EDUCATION FUNDING

A young couple in their late 20s have a toddler and another child on the way. Their joint income is £35,000. While keeping tax to a minimum they want a

CHARGES

Charges can have quite an effect on PEP performance. PEPs with high setting-up costs will suffer in the early stages of the plan. That is why PEPs must be seen as long-term investments.

There are many possible types of charge which can be levied on a PEP. There is a big difference between funds (unit trusts and

Examples continued

general home for savings in order to build up a nest egg for future needs – particularly for school or university fees.

They decide to start a PEP each, saving a total of £150 a month. They choose two different management groups: an investment trust manager with a history of good performance, and a unit trust manager with a big range of funds, including PEP funds with no front-end charge. They plan to start with lower risk, general funds and move into more aggressive growth funds, such as smaller companies, as their portfolio builds.

GOING ABROAD
Over a period of years an investor has sheltered around £60,000 of savings in PEPs. He has avoided high-risk homes for his money, choosing mainly UK income and index tracker funds and blue chip shares.

His adviser suggests that a wider international spread would be a good idea, since at present his whole investment exposure is to the UK market. He decides therefore to concentrate his current year's general PEP allowance on overseas funds, choosing a manager with a good range of international funds. He puts £3,000 into the manager's

award-winning European fund, which does not invest in the UK, £1,500 into an international fund which has more than 50% in the UK, and £1,500 (the maximum allowed) into a non-qualifying fund which invests in smaller Asian markets. The end result is a portfolio which has only about one-fifth in the UK.

BEGINNER'S CHOICE
A woman aged 33, on her own after a divorce, has returned to work and is trying to build up her savings. She is new to stockmarket investment and wants to keep risk to a minimum. She reads an article about 'toe in the water' investment in PEPs, and considers some of the suggested choices. She looks at a UK index tracker fund, which offers relatively steady performance with low volatility, but decides in the end on a well-known international investment trust which has 70% of its portfolio in the UK.

It also has a wide spread of international investments, including small percentages in riskier areas like smaller companies and emerging markets. She feels it offers a complete 'portfolio in miniature' for a novice investor and is also attracted by its low charges and low minimum investment.

PERSONAL EQUITY PLANS

investment trusts) and shares which are held directly. Funds carry their own charges, but the PEP manager may impose an additional PEP charge for 'packaging' the investment. You should avoid plans which do this.

Some PEPs have a PEP charge (initial and/or annual) but then drop the fund charges. You can only work this out by reading the small print very carefully. PEPs which comprise funds and shares in one plan usually even out the charges. They might have no additional PEP charge on the funds, but may add one to the equity holdings.

Shares do not carry annual management charges, so managed share PEPs usually add this sort of charge to the package. They may also add an initial charge – sometimes quite high. It may be that by holding shares through a PEP you are incurring costs equal to those of a unit trust.

Shares, on the other hand, unlike unit trusts, do have dealing charges: the broker's commission for each purchase and sale. These also vary a lot in PEPs. A big organisation dealing in large sums may be able to reduce dealing costs to a negligible amount – say 0·2% – but some companies, particularly private client stockbrokers, may charge up to 2%. Remember that this is a charge on buying and selling shares. If your PEP is managed by the broker concerned, it is up to that person how often he or she buys and sells – so you cannot directly control costs.

Some PEPs have a fixed-rate initial charge instead of a percentage charge. This will usually favour the larger investor and may make the PEP impractical for someone with only £1,000 to invest. Beware the 'fixed charge per holding' arrangement. This may be fine if you have a fairly large investment in only one share or fund. It would look quite different if your PEP was spread across several different holdings.

Some PEP managers pay higher than normal commissions to advisers. This is likely to result in higher initial charges. An expensive way to buy a PEP may be to go through an adviser who will then put you into a PEP which is actually run by a different plan manager.

A number of major unit trust groups have PEPs with no initial charge, but a redemption charge if you close your PEP in the first few years.

For instance, you might pay 4·5% on redemptions in the first year, which will then taper down to 1% in the fifth year. Redemption charges should not be a cause for concern for the PEP investor who is happy to leave his or her money invested for the long term. PEPs with no initial charge usually have only one fund link – often an index tracker fund or a special managed portfolio.

PEP PERFORMANCE

The main reason for holding a PEP is to have an investment which will offer a good return over a period of years. Performance is therefore important, and should not be lost sight of among the array of different PEPs, many of which offer special discounts to entice you in.

It is impossible to assess the performance of many of the managed PEPs, especially those in which an individual portfolio is run for you by an adviser. However, funds which are 'PEPable' can be checked up on. You can keep an eye on unit trust and investment trust PEP performance through figures reported in the specialist press – but make sure you are comparing investments over the same period, and remember that PEP figures should be shown 'gross income reinvested' (that is, with no tax deduction on dividends), whereas most fund performance figures are given with 'net income reinvested'.

If your PEP performance is disappointing it is possible to transfer a PEP from one fund manager to another – and you may be tempted to do so, especially under pressure from an adviser or an inviting advert.

Transfers are to be avoided unless you have really lost faith in your existing manager and feel that performance problems are not caused merely by a temporary blip. There may be an exit charge on your old PEP, and don't forget that you will suffer the bid/offer spread as well.

A PEP with no front-end cost but an early redemption charge will have quite a sting in the tail if you want to transfer out, though it will be attractive for transferring in. Most new plan managers will also have an initial charge or dealing costs, though some groups offer special discounts to investors who want to transfer.

If you want to transfer part of your PEP account to another manager you may be in for a shock. Some managers merge several years' PEP savings into one account. If this is how your plan is administered, you can only transfer the account as a whole.

This is a nuisance if your reason for transferring is not total disillusionment with your PEP provider, but merely a wish to move your money into a different type of PEP fund. For example, you might have a strong UK portfolio, but you want to spread your money into international funds, and your current manager doesn't offer the sort of fund you want.

There is no way round this problem, though you could just consider moving your next year's PEP contribution to a new manager and leaving your existing account where it is.

To give yourself maximum flexibility at the outset, choose a manager with a good performance record in more than one investment sector, and a number of alternative funds for your PEP money. It is easy to switch between funds run by the same manager, and there should be a discount on this type of switch.

If you want to transfer your PEP, there is just one golden rule: start by approaching the manager you want to transfer to. He or she will give you a simple form to fill in. The new manager then arranges the transfer with the old manager. You must not try to arrange the transfer yourself by realising your PEP and taking the cash to a new manager. If you do this you will invalidate the PEP and lose access to that year's tax-free allowance.

WOULD YOU BENEFIT FROM A PEP?

Some people have argued that the tax benefits due from PEPs are not all that significant. The dividends paid out on most equity funds are relatively low, so the income tax saving doesn't really amount to that much. The allowances and exempt limits on capital gains tax mean that few people pay it anyway, and it is easy to avoid by 'bed and breakfasting' your holding (see Chapter 10). With some PEPs, setting up charges could even outweigh the tax benefits.

This argument might make sense in some circumstances. For instance, a small investor expecting to leave money invested for only five years would be unwise to put it into a PEP with high charges investing purely for growth. However, someone investing only £30 a month over ten years in an income unit trust which has no PEP charges in addition to the standard trust charges should benefit.

Charges in the PEP market began to fall in the mid-1990s, and there are now a lot of plans to choose from which have low or no entry costs. Some fund management groups make it cheaper to buy their funds with a PEP than without one.

The graphs on pages 122 and 123 show the advantages built into PEPs. In practice PEPs are a worthwhile investment for many, if not most, investors. Higher-rate taxpayers will clearly get the most benefit from a PEP, particularly if they have taxable capital gains.

For lower-rate taxpayers the benefits are less obvious – but could be considerable over the long term. If you are not paying higher-rate tax you can enhance your benefits by investing for income. Choosing a low-cost PEP will help. High front-end charges are damaging to your investment in its early years.

Independent financial adviser and *Moneywise* Ask the Professionals panellist Keith Sanham says:

"A non-taxpayer could have a PEP providing charges are neutral. An advantage is that the tax is reclaimed by the PEP manager so it saves you the administrative hassle."

PEPs bring no tax advantage for non-taxpayers. But there may be reasons for the non-taxpayer to consider them:

○ Your income may be close to the tax-free limit. An additional investment could generate extra income that makes you a taxpayer.
○ You may be uncertain whether you will pay tax in the future.
○ You may wish to put your money in an investment offered through a PEP, such as an income portfolio or corporate bond.
○ Your investment may be offered more cheaply through the PEP than outside it.
○ PEPs are as easy to buy and run as unit trusts or investment trusts and do not need to be declared on your tax return.

Arguably there are some categories of investor for whom PEPs are not suitable. Anyone who could not tolerate the risk of a share investment should not have a PEP. This includes those with small amounts of capital who can't afford to risk a fall in share price or who will need to get at their money in less than ten years.

It would also be possible to damage your wealth by choosing the wrong kind of PEP. A small investor with no other share-type investments would be ill-advised to have only a single company PEP. A unit trust or investment trust PEP investing in general funds and offering a spread of risk would be much better.

An inexperienced investor would be better off choosing a managed or discretionary PEP than trying to make his or her own choices through a self select plan. Though direct shareholdings offer their own special sort of excitement, the small investor would be much safer investing through funds.

How to buy a PEP

SOME KNOWLEDGE IS NEEDED to distinguish one PEP from another, but the business of investing is quite simple. PEPs can be bought by sending an application through the post to the PEP manager, or as a result of face-to-face consultation with a financial adviser or with a stockbroker.

A simple unit trust or investment trust PEP can be started with very little formality. If you ask a stockbroker to manage a discretionary PEP for you, you will need to spend some time discussing your needs.

You will be sent statements twice a year with most plans, though managers will usually supply an extra statement free on request, or you can ask for a current valuation over the phone.

When you make your investment you must use a personal cheque – not, for example, one from your business account if you run your own company.

There is always a bulge in PEP investment towards the end of the tax year, as the deadline for using that year's PEP allowance approaches. If you leave your PEP investment until late in the year, remember that the deadline for your chosen plan manager could be earlier than the last day of the tax year (5th April). Plan managers often need a few extra days to process applications. Make sure that you check up on your deadline well ahead of time.

Q&A

Q Will I get reports and accounts of companies I invest in through my PEP?

A Not automatically. Your PEP manager may arrange it for you if you want, though a fee will probably be charged. If you invest in unit trusts or investment trusts you won't get reports and accounts for companies held in the portfolio.

Q I have shares in a number of blue chip companies. Can they be transferred into a PEP?

A Your shares cannot be transferred into the PEP. They will have to be sold and bought back within the plan. This operation is known as a 'bed and PEP' (compare 'Bed and breakfast' – see Chapter 10) and your PEP manager may be able to offer favourable dealing terms.

Q I am self-employed and usually wait until the end of the tax year to invest, when I see how much free cash I have available. Is there any disadvantage to this?

A Provided you get your cheque in on time there is no particular disadvantage, except that the earlier your money goes in, the more time it has to grow. There may be an advantage in waiting if you are looking at a new type of fund, and expect more to be launched as the year goes on. Why not choose a PEP at the start of the year and invest a relatively small monthly amount, then top up with a lump sum when you can afford it at the year end.

Action plan

○ Work through the flowcharts on pages 128 and 131.

○ Choose a number of possible PEPs which fit your broad requirements or approach a financial adviser for further information.

○ Make sure the management group or the stockbroker you choose has a strong performance record in the sector which interests you. Check funds against industry performance categories as a whole. Don't rely on claims from the groups – these can be manipulated to sound good. Stockbroker performance is more problematic (see Chapter 9), but a switched-on broker should have a performance yardstick which will help assess investment performance.

○ Keep as much flexibility as possible. If you think you might build up a sizeable fund and need to spread your investments, choose a manager with a range of funds on offer.

○ Check on deadlines near the tax year-end. Don't let a regular savings PEP run over the year end if you are intending to move in the next year to another manager.

○ Check that your cheque is the right sort for PEP purposes.

○ Monitor your investment every few months, but don't be panicked into an expensive transfer.

139

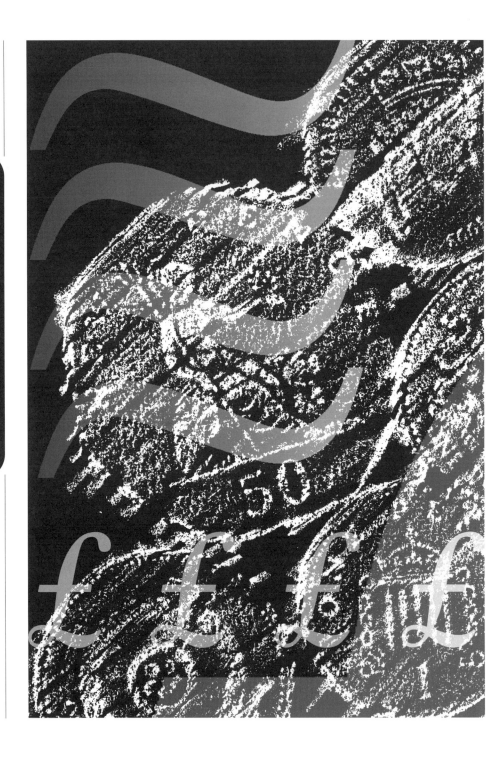

8
Gilts and other investments

This chapter covers some other types of investment that can be traded and which may be suitable for part of your investment portfolio. The first section looks at fixed-interest investments and the second at the riskiest end of the spectrum – derivatives.

Independent Financial Adviser and *Moneywise* Ask the Professionals panellist Keith Sanham says:

"Gilts can perform a useful function within a portfolio, particularly if a steady and predictable level of income is required. But a knowledge of the market is essential as the attraction or otherwise of a particular stock does vary depending on market conditions."

Gilts are another well-known investment that can be bought through the stockmarket. They are among a range of securities known as 'fixed-interest investments' or 'bonds'.

The concept of fixed interest is simple: you get a fixed return on your money, unlike most building society and bank accounts where the return is variable. The level of return is usually higher than that of share dividends, and in times of low interest rates it may be higher than bank and building society rates as well.

But fixed interest is actually a highly technical type of investment, not easily accessible to the private investor. All fixed-interest securities are loans: government stocks, or gilts – the most important class of fixed interest – are loans raised by the government.

Gilts originated in the 17th century when William III's government wanted to finance its war against France. The loan concept proved so useful it is still with us today. For investors the interest paid on the stock provides a steady return, offering very high security since, in effect, the British Government cannot go bankrupt.

HOW GILTS WORK

The government wants to raise money and so it issues a new gilt. The public agrees to lend money to the government by buying stock from the new issue.

The government promises to pay back the loan (the amount originally invested) at a particular date some years in the future (known as the 'redemption date'). In the interim, it will pay a dividend twice a year at an annual rate of interest (the 'coupon') which is agreed at the outset and fixed for the life of the stock. The amount of the coupon will reflect interest rates at the time.

The gilt issue is sold in notional 'units' of £100. For every £100 issued (£100 'nominal') the holder of the stock will get £100 back (the 'par value') on the redemption date.

The name of the gilt issue will tell you the coupon and the year in which the stock matures. For example, Treasury 13% 2000 pays interest of 13% per £100 nominal of stock, to be redeemed at par on 14 July 2000. It was issued in June 1980, when base rates stood at 17%.

Because of its high coupon, and also because it was trading 'cum dividend', this stock was priced at £115 25/32 in July 1997 (see table on page 145).

Gilts with less than five years to redemption are called short-dated, those with five to fifteen years are medium-dated and those with more than fifteen years to go are long-dated – abbreviated to shorts, mediums and longs.

Unlike most loans, government securities can be traded on the stockmarket. In other words, one lender can sell his or her stock on to another. The person buying the stock then becomes entitled to receive the dividends and the value of the stock at the redemption date. As the stock is traded, the price of the gilt can go up and down, so the seller of the stock may make a loss or a profit on the sale of a holding.

Suppose the stock has a coupon of 10%. This means it will pay out £10 for each £100 nominal of stock. If the buyer pays only £90 for each £100 nominal, the true yield from his or her point of view has changed: a dividend of £10 on an investment of £90 gives a yield of 11%. If the purchase cost had been £105, the result would have been a yield of 9·5%. This yield figure is known as the 'flat yield' or 'interim yield'. It may also be called the 'interest yield' or the 'income yield'. To calculate the flat yield the coupon is divided by the current price. Price and yield are clearly linked: if the price rises, the yield will fall; if it falls, the yield will rise. The price is a mechanism for adjusting the gilt yield to bring it more in line with current market rates.

EXAMPLE

An investor buys a gilt with a coupon of 7%. He invests £5,000 at £95 per £100 nominal. If he holds on to it until it is redeemed, he knows exactly what he will be getting: £100 back on redemption for every £100 nominal of stock bought, and also £7 per £100 nominal every year in dividends until the end of the term. He will actually receive a total of £368 in dividends each year (a flat yield of 7·4%). He will also get £5 capital growth for every £95 invested, giving him his capital back plus a gain of £263 on redemption. The beauty is that once locked in, this return is fully guaranteed.

What causes a price change in a gilt? Gilts are sensitive to political events which might affect the economic climate, but above all they react to interest rates. Since a gilt is a fixed-interest stock, it will look most attractive when interest rates generally are low or falling. Rising interest rates will make deposit accounts look more profitable than gilts, so gilts will be less popular. What happens is that the market automatically adjusts the gilt price so that the yield is competitive. If interest rates rise then gilt yields will rise too, and gilt prices will fall. If interest rates fall, gilt yields will follow, and gilt prices will go up.

Because of this interplay between price and yield, there are two possible kinds of return on a gilt: income, from the six-monthly dividend, and capital growth, from the price change. The combined effect of the two sources of return is shown in the redemption yield, which takes into account any capital gain or loss on maturity.

QUICK GUIDE TO READING GILTS:

- If the price you pay is more than £100 you will make a loss when the gilt reaches maturity. If the price is less than £100 you will make a gain.
- If the flat yield is higher than the redemption yield, you will make a capital loss on maturity. If the redemption yield is higher, you will make a gain.

VARIABLE YIELDS

If you look at the daily price data on gilts (they are listed in the *Financial Times*, and in other national newspapers) you will find that the coupon varies a good deal from one stock to another, but the redemption yields will be fairly similar. In mid-1997, with the base rate at 6·5%, gilt redemption yields ranged from 6·5% to just over 7%.

At these levels gilt yields were seen as attractive, so most gilts were trading at above par value (that is, at more than £100 for each £100 nominal of stock). The price of short-dated gilts, as the table opposite shows, tends to move towards par value as the redemption date approaches.

INDEX-LINKED GILTS

In addition to 'conventional' stocks there are also gilt issues whose purpose is to protect the investor from inflation.

With these, both the coupon and the par value are linked to the Retail Price Index, so they give a growing income plus a small extra percentage yield and on redemption they give you back your capital enhanced in line with inflation.

Index-linked gilts are hard to assess because a major component of the return – that is, inflation – is unpredictable. In mid-1997 most stocks were expected to give a real return of around 3.5% – that is, 3.5% over and above inflation – assuming the RPI goes up steadily by 5%.

One problem is that during the life of the stock the price goes up and down in response to stockmarket sentiment, and will not necessarily reflect the built-in enhancement of the stock's value in line with inflation. The full inflation enhancement is only guaranteed on redemption.

Index-linked stocks are worth considering by the smaller investor who wants part of his or her savings to be inflation-linked, though he or she should buy and hold to maturity unless advised by a stockbroker. Index-linked gilts are specially suitable to higher rate taxpayers but not to non-taxpayers.

The figures in the table opposite show why: compared to a conventional gilt the 'break-even' inflation rate is two or three times higher for a non-taxpayer than for a 40% taxpayer.

TAX AND GILTS

You must pay tax on the income from a gilt (though gilt yields are usually quoted gross, or without a deduction for tax), but any capital growth on gilts is tax free. When looking at yields for indi-

GILTS: SAMPLE PRICES AND YIELDS AT 1 JULY 1997

Yields shown are gross. Net yields show returns for 20% and 40% taxpayers.

	Price	Flat yield %	Redemption yield %	Net yield 20%	Net yield 40%
SHORTS					
Treasury 13% 2000	$115^{25}/_{32}$	11.228	7.138	4.763	2.385
Treasury 7% 2001	$99^{19}/_{32}$	7.029	7.099	5.697	4.296
MEDIUMS					
Treasury $6^3/_4$% 2004	$96^3/_{32}$	6.881	7.079	5.714	4.350
Treasury 9% 2008	$114^7/_{32}$	7.880	7.139	5.489	3.833
LONGS					
Treasury 8% 2015	$108^{26}/_{32}$	7.352	7.132	5.624	4.112
INDEX-LINKED					
Breakeven inflation rate*		0%	20%	40%	
$2^1/_2$% 2003	$182^{15}/_{32}$	3.28	2.14	1.00	
$2^1/_2$% 2013	$147^{28}/_{32}$	3.44	2.44	1.44	

shows the minimum inflation rate needed for the index-linked stock to give a higher return than a conventional comparison stock.

Source: MoneyFacts

vidual stocks, remember that they are usually shown gross (without any deduction for tax).

GILT STRATEGIES

There are gilts, or combinations of gilts, appropriate to all financial circumstances, but choosing a strategy will also depend on market conditions. The investor in the example on page 146, for example, could not have used this particular strategy in mid-1997, because gilts were mostly trading above par after a long period of low interest rates.

After a period of rising interest rates, the price of low coupon stocks has fallen substantially. A higher-rate taxpayer takes the opportunity to invest. Though the interim yield, because of the low coupon, is small, the redemption yield will be high thanks to the capital gain on maturity.

Capital gains in gilts are not taxable. This is good news for the higher-rate taxpayer who does not want highly taxed dividends, but is better served by tax-free capital gains.

The basic-rate taxpayer should steer a course somewhere between the two examples opposite, depending on how much income is required. Though the principles of choosing a gilt are easy, the actual choice is another matter. Taxpayers, especially, should seek advice from a stockbroker.

EXAMPLE
An elderly investor has savings of £15,000. She badly needs an income boost. She has no provision for growth of either income or capital. Her stockbroker recommends a small portfolio of gilts, chosen with varying distribution dates (so as to give her a monthly income), and priced at or below par (to preserve her capital). This is not the ideal solution to her problem: it does not provide for capital growth, and as the gilts are redeemed they will have to be replaced with new stocks, possibly at a time when yields are lower.

Choosing a gilt to hold to redemption is risk-free in that the return is absolutely predictable. But if you sell before the redemption date you are at the mercy of market prices. You may be able to use this to your advantage, but this sort of trading is generally only for those who follow the market or who are getting investment advice.

The performance of gilts is not usually as dramatic as that of equities, though there are moments when the gilt market can take off. In 1982, for example, the UK economy was just coming out of a deep recession. The government had cut interest rates and allowed the pound to fall. Gilts had just been through a bad patch. With the oil price shock and high inflation at the end of the 1970s, yields had become unsustainably high – as inflation and interest rates came down, the gilt market saw returns of 40% or more.

This sort of performance, however, is highly exceptional. Over the long term, gilts have not done nearly as well for investors as have equities. The BZW Long-term Equity-Gilt study shows that someone putting £100 into equities in 1945 would have seen their money grow to £59,157 by the end of 1996, or £2,806 after taking inflation into account. The same investment in gilts would have produced £2,095, or £99 after inflation.

Looking back as far as 1918, the average rate of return after inflation for equities was 7·86% a year. For gilts it was 1·97 % and for cash (deposit investments) 1·48%. The average dividend yield on shares over the period was 5·1%; on bonds (fixed-interest investments) it was 6·7%.

The message here is that although gilts may be useful for specific purposes, such as the provision of income, they are not likely to do any better than shares in companies over a long investment period. They are of use to investors who wish to shelter capital from equity market fluctuations, but they should not make up the majority of a growth portfolio.

There is a further problem for income investors which is touched on in the example, left. If an investor locks into a fixed income from gilts, and inflation and interest rates take off, the income they are receiving will be left behind. But the investor will find it difficult to realise his or her capital and seek another investment with a higher yield, because the rising rates would make gilt prices fall, eroding the investor's capital. For further guidance on whether to buy, you should use the flowchart on page 148.

Q&A

Q *Is there a minimum investment in gilts?*

A No, but like shares the charges involved in dealing through stockbrokers may discourage anything less than, say, £1,000. It is worth dealing in smaller amounts through the National Savings

Should you invest in gilts?

Do you need immediate guaranteed income?

- **Yes** →
- **No** → **Do you already have some growth investments?**

Is long-term growth of income an essential?

- **Yes** →
- **No** →

Do you already have some growth investments?

- **Yes** →
- **No** → Take advice or review your whole portfolio – you need some growth investment in addition to gilts.

Yes (long-term growth essential): You should not put all your capital into gilts but should seek a proper growth vehicle for part or all of it.

Will you hold to redemption or will you need access to your money before then?

- Access needed
- Hold to redemption →

Are you able to sacrifice some capital for a higher income?

- **Yes** → You could consider stocks trading at over £100 ('above par').
- **No** → You should consider stocks trading at £100 or less ('below par').

Access needed: There is a risk of capital loss if you have to sell when gilt prices are low.

What is your tax status?

- Non taxpayer: Choose the highest yielding gilt with a suitable redemption date trading at £100 or less.
- Lower-rate taxpayer: Choose stocks offering a balance of income and growth.

Do you need monthly income?

- **Yes** → Choose gilts at a suitable yield and price with a combination of dividend dates to give regular income. You should hold to maturity for a guaranteed return.
- **No** → Gilts are suitable. Choose the highest yield available at an acceptable price. You should hold to maturity for a guaranteed return.

Do you expect interest rates to go up?

- **Yes** → Avoid gilts.
- **No** → Invest with caution.

Higher-rate taxpayer: Choose low coupon stocks with high redemption yields.

Stock Register. You could also consider investing through a unit trust. For further details on both, see below.

Q *Why do commentators usually recommend short- or medium-dated gilts? Surely it would be best to lock into the longest possible term?*

A Stockbrokers usually advise shorts or mediums because the price fluctuates less than long-dated stocks. If you buy a stock with a 20-year life there is a good chance you may want to sell it before redemption, and an increased possibility that the price may fall significantly.

Q *Why do you see gilt prices like '106$^{15}/_{32}$'?*

A Being such a traditional investment, gilts are surrounded by quaint terminology and anomalies. It is simply a tradition that prices are quoted in sixteenths or thirty-seconds – though how much longer this will last in the face of computer technology remains to be seen.

Q *I bought some gilts through a stockbroker and now I want to sell. I see that the rates through the National Savings Stock Register are much cheaper. Can I sell that way?*

A No. You have to sell through the same route as you bought.

How to buy gilts

There are two ways to buy gilts directly: through a stockbroker or through the National Savings Stock Register. You can also buy gilts through a unit trust – but not through a PEP, as gilts are not 'PEPable'.

1 *Stockbrokers*

   The advantage of a stockbroker is that you can get advice on which stock to buy, though not all stockbrokers will handle very small purchases. The disadvantages are:

   ○ *Charges* A stockbroker will have a minimum charge which may be £25 or more per stock purchased. This makes it an expensive way to deal for small investors. Telephone services may offer cheaper dealing for small sums, but will not give advice. However, any broker can tell you the current price when you put in your order.

○ *Dividends* If you buy through a stockbroker, the dividends will be paid to you after deduction of tax at 20%. This is inconvenient if you are a non-taxpayer, as it means you have to reclaim the tax paid from the Inland Revenue each year. If you pay tax at a higher rate than 20%, you will have to pay the difference. If you are not a regular client with the stockbroker, dividends will be paid by warrant (like a cheque), which you have to pay into your bank account.

2 *National Savings Stock Register (NSSR)*
This is a very cheap and efficient way to buy, with costs of only £12.50 minimum or 0·7% for deals of up to £5,000. You can get the order forms from larger branches of the Post Office or from the Bonds and Stock Office, Blackpool, FY3 9YP; tel. 0253 697333 (24 hours). The disadvantages are:
○ You have to choose your own stock.
○ You deal by post, so you won't know the dealing price on the spot. In practice this is not a problem for the smaller investor.
   The disadvantages of the NSSR are far outweighed by its advantages: cheapness, simplicity of dealing, and the fact that dividends are paid gross direct into your bank account.
   Whether you buy through the Post Office or direct, don't forget that if you buy when the stock is ex-dividend (xd) you will not get the next dividend payment, which will go to the stock's seller. The buying price will be a little lower to reflect this.

GILT INVESTMENT FUNDS
A gilt investment fund, which may be either a UK unit trust or a fund registered offshore, invests in a pooled portfolio of gilts in order to give access to the market and management expertise to the smaller investor. The advantages are that someone else is choosing the stocks, and there are no maturity dates to worry about. The investment can be either for growth or for income. Remember that if you choose a gilt income fund the yield is not fixed in the same way as that of an individual stock holding. It may vary over the course of time, though it should not move by much.
   There are several points to consider if you are thinking of a fund.
○ *Charges*: Gilt funds levy charges, making them more expensive than dealing direct. Look for management groups which have kept their gilt fund charges low.

- *Performance*: Check the historical performance of the fund. There is no point in investing in one which cannot improve on buying direct.
- *Tax*: A pure gilt fund, like any UK unit trust, can give rise to a capital gains tax bill. Therefore, if you have a large holding of gilts which might give rise to a gain in excess of your annual tax-free limit, the fund could create a liability where none would have existed if you had held the gilts directly. In practice this should not be a major concern for the smaller investor.
- *Capital erosion*: A fund manager can increase the yield on the fund by buying gilts whose price is above par, so that they will make a loss on maturity. In other words, capital is being sacrificed to produce a high income. The fund's value could fall through the use of such methods, and the fund could end up having to cut its dividends. Income-seeking investor should be aware of this problem: the fund's management objectives should make it clear whether this type of strategy will be used, and funds offering a much higher yield than average should be avoided. This has been a danger in the past with offshore gilt funds, but may also affect unit trusts.

Other fixed-interest investments

THERE ARE A NUMBER of different types of fixed-interest stock apart from gilts. Fixed-interest stocks are issued by governments, government agencies, companies and building societies.

Corporate bonds (stocks issued by companies) have become much better known since their inclusion in PEPs was first permitted in 1995. They can be held directly by investors within a PEP, though the bulk of corporate bond PEP investment is through unit trusts (see Chapter 5).

All fixed-interest investments work in a similar way to gilts: they have a coupon and a fluctuating share price which affects the yield in the hands of the investor. They mostly have a limited life.

As with gilts, you will get a predetermined return if you hold on to redemption, and you might make a loss or a profit if you sell before the stock is redeemed.

With any loan stock there is a risk that the issuer of the stock will go bankrupt, in which case the investment would be a total loss. This risk is not a major worry with gilts, or with many other government stocks: there is very little likelihood that the government of a developed country will go bust.

With corporate bonds the issue is of a little more concern. Though a major blue chip company may run little risk of failure, the same is not true for all companies that issue bonds. To give investors some idea of the financial soundness of companies, they are given credit ratings by special rating agencies.

A rating of AAA ('triple A') from Standard & Poors denotes the strongest bond issuers, while a CCC rating means there is a real possibility that the company could go bust. Issuers with less than top notch credit ratings will have to issue bonds with higher yields to persuade investors to take on the risk.

Independent financial adviser and *Moneywise* Ask the Professionals panellist Keith Sanham says:

"Corporate bond PEPs are particularly useful for those requiring a moderately high level of income and who are little concerned with retaining the purchasing power of the capital , that is, when income is more important than capital growth. But, too high a yield can be a warning that funds are riskier than gilts so they should ideally be selected where the yield gives scope for some capital growth over the longer term."

TYPES OF STOCK

○ *Debentures*: These are fixed-interest bonds which are secured on the company's assets in the same way as your home is security for your mortgage. If the issuer went into liquidation the debenture holders would have the first call on the assets specified as security to repay the loan.

Debentures are the safest type of stock in the pecking order for repayment, because they are secured on company assets. Because of their relatively low risk, the yields will be relatively low. Their prices move in a similar way to those of gilts, though debenture prices will also reflect the health of the issuing company.

○ *Loan stocks*: Like debentures, but unsecured and therefore more risky, but with correspondingly higher yields.

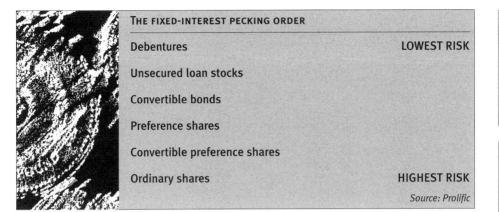

THE FIXED-INTEREST PECKING ORDER	
Debentures	LOWEST RISK
Unsecured loan stocks	
Convertible bonds	
Preference shares	
Convertible preference shares	
Ordinary shares	HIGHEST RISK

Source: Prolific

○ *Convertibles*: In structure these may be either bonds or preference shares. Bonds are the safer of the two. These stocks are
called convertibles because at a specified date (or dates) in the
future they can be converted into the same company's ordinary
shares at a fixed price. The coupon is usually lower than
on a non-convertible bond, to take account of the extra benefit of conversion rights, but it will be higher than on the ordinary shares.

Because of their link to the ordinary shares convertible
price movements can follow those of the ordinary shares. But
as an income stock, convertibles should be protected from a
major fall in the ordinary share price.

○ *Preference shares*: These are not loan capital like the other
types of stock, but form part of the ordinary share capital of
the issuer. They have some special features, of which a fixed
dividend is the most important. Some have a conversion option
attached. Most have no redemption date.

Dividends are often cumulative: if the company cannot pay
them in one year, it must add them on to the next year's payment. Because there is no repayment date the investor does not
know when the loan will be repaid. This adds to the risk,
which in turn means relatively high yields.

In the event of an issuer's collapse, all the different securities it has in issue are allotted a pecking order. This lays down
which stocks will be paid off first, second and so on. Some
companies may have a number of types of stock in issue, so the
picture can get complicated (see the section on split capital

investment trusts in Chapter 6). A pecking order of fixed-interest stocks in order of repayment ranking is shown on page 153.

○ *Building society shares*: Permanent interest-bearing shares, or PIBs, are another type of fixed-interest stock which is suitable for use by the private investor, though a number of the stocks on offer are sold in very large units, which effectively prevents smaller investors from buying.

PIBs are shares which were issued by the building societies before demutualisation was an issue. They offer a relatively high fixed yield and, like gilts, pay interest twice a year.

PIBs are irredeemable, so although the interest is fixed, unfortunately there is no way of knowing what your capital return will be: investors are dependent on market conditions when they decide to sell. PIBs come last in the repayment order if the building society is wound up, and the issuing society could miss a payment and not be obliged to roll it up for payment at a later date.

All these factors make PIBs more risky than many types of fixed interest, though some are issued by very substantial societies, which are unlikely to run into difficulties. A stockbroker who specialises in these stocks can give you details of current prices and yields.

Derivatives

IF GILTS ARE ONE OF THE SAFEST homes for your money, derivatives, in at least some of their aspects, take the prize for being the most risky.

Derivatives originated over a century ago in Chicago with commodities contracts designed to help producers and traders protect themselves against big price movements. The two parties would agree a sale at a specified price to take place at a future date.

Eventually it was realised that as well as protection, this kind of futures trading could also be used for speculation – effectively betting on price movements for pure profit.

Commodity futures, which cover everything from aluminium to potatoes, are still flourishing, though because of contract sizes and

Independent financial adviser and *Moneywise* Ask the Professionals panellist Rebekah Kearey says:

"Derivatives are investments which are tied to an 'artificial' concept, such as a stock index, rather than to stocks and shares themselves. They are often used as part of the underlying portfolio for investment products with guarantees. For example, investment bonds which guarantee your money back as a minimum return plus X% 'income' a year, and unit trusts which lock into increases in the FTSE 100 every four months, use derivatives to create the guarantee."

the nature of the market itself they are not a practical proposition for the private investor.

The modern trend has been towards financial futures, where investors can make bets on future movements in things like interest rates, the FTSE 100 Index, and foreign currencies. Financial futures are also unlikely to appeal to most private investors, as the potential losses if you get it wrong are enormous. However, they are used by companies offering relatively common investments like tracker trusts and funds which guarantee the return of your original investment. They are traded at the London International Financial Futures and Options Exchange (LIFFE).

Traded options have all the excitement of derivatives contracts, but are accessible to private investors with relatively small amounts of money to invest. Traded options are option contracts on the shares of individual companies. In July 1997, there were options available on 75 companies.

An option is a contract which gives you the right, but not the obligation, to deal in the shares of the company concerned. Contracts which give the right to buy are 'call options'. If you want the right to sell you buy a 'put option'. The option specifies the quantity to be traded, the price, and the period during which the deal can be done. The price is known as the 'exercise' or 'strike' price and the last day on which you can cash in the option is called the 'expiry date'.

Options are geared investments: you don't have to put up the whole investment initially to get the full return. The cost of the option is called the 'premium'. For a blue chip company in steady trading conditions it will cost 7–10% of the share price. For example, a blue chip company whose shares trade at 450p may have three-month options at 36p per share with an exercise price of 500p.

Option contracts specify a minimum number of shares – typically 1,000 – so one contract would cost £360. This is the most the investor could lose, unlike some futures contracts where losses can be unlimited. For the investor to make a profit, the share price would have to go above 486p (the price of the shares plus the option premium).

If the shares actually went up to 550p within the life of the options, the investor would have made 64p – a profit of almost 200% on the original 36p stake. If he or she had bought the shares themselves the price increase would have brought a 22% return.

If the shares fell below 450p, the option would expire without value and the investor would lose his or her premium. But if they started to fall gradually the investor could sell the options contract and get back some of the investment.

A put option is a bet on a fall in share prices. It can be used to hedge the risk on a share portfolio if you think the market might fall: what you lose you make up for with gains on the option.

These are the simplest kind of options strategies and are relatively low-risk. There are much more complex, high-risk strategies which should only be attempted by those experienced in the financial markets. For private investors who want to learn more about options, there are brokers who specialise in the area, and offer advice – many work on an execution-only basis. The Internet also has many web sites which give further information about the subject.

You might also hear about 'swaps'. These are agreements between two or more parties to swap sets of cash flows over a pre-set period. Swaps can be set up against the value of interest on debt – this would be known as an interest rate swap. At its simplest, one party in an interest rate swap holds a fixed-rate debt instrument and the other has a variable rate of interest from its holdings. For business reasons, the parties want to exchange these rates of interest.

Swaps cannot be traded on an exchange. They are set up as 'over-the-counter' deals by the large investment houses. Because there is no central exchange the swaps market is unregulated and some experts worry about the extent of unsecured risk taken by banks and finance firms.

INDIRECT INVESTMENT IN DERIVATIVES

You may already be investing in derivatives indirectly. Pension funds use derivatives to manage the spread of their investment. It is up to the trustees of each pension fund to oversee and approve the investment spread, so each manager should agree guidelines with the trustees.

Unit trust managers are allowed to use exchange-traded futures and options contracts for portfolio management. If you invest in a tracker fund you may find that costs have been kept down by buying futures.

Investment trust managers can use derivatives in the same way as unit trust managers, including hedging the portfolio against the risk of falling share prices.

Action plan

○ Remember you need to have a spread of types of investment – you shouldn't put all your money in direct investment in shares.

○ Use the flowchart on page 148 to work out whether gilts would be suitable for you, and if so, the type you should invest in.

○ Get to grips with the way other fixed-interest type investments work.

○ If you're looking for income, check whether a corporate bond PEP would make sense.

○ If you're prepared to take a lot of risk in the hope of higher returns, you could try derivatives. But be sure you understand how they work first and what the worst case scenario would be.

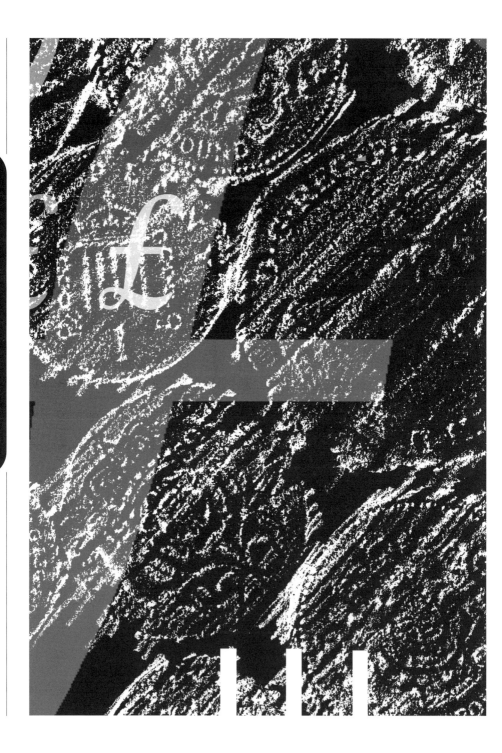

9 Stockbroker services

The stockbroking profession has been around for a long time – much longer than that of the insurance-oriented independent financial adviser (IFA). There were brokers dealing in the shares of companies in coffee houses even before 1773 when the Stock Exchange itself was founded.

In the last ten years there has been a revolution in financial services, and stockbroking is changing along with everything else. Though they have traditionally been seen as serving only very wealthy investors, most private client stockbrokers will deal in a friendly and helpful way with first-time enquirers, and many welcome clients with relatively small portfolios.

Membership of the Stock Exchange is a prerequisite in order to deal in shares. In addition to their Stock Exchange membership, stockbrokers now have to be regulated under the Financial Services Act. Their regulator is the Securities and Futures Authority (SFA).

TYPES OF STOCKBROKER

There are three main types of stockbroker. The distinguishing factor is the nature of the client they deal with.

○ *Institutional stockbrokers* buy and sell shares mainly on behalf of big clients like pension funds and insurance companies. They may also have a private client department, but it will usually deal only with larger clients – which might mean an absolute minimum of £250,000 or more.

Institutional brokers will also sponsor share issues – that is, they advise companies on how to issue their shares on the stockmarket, and do their best to make sure the issue is a success with the market. They also have big research departments whose job is to follow different companies or market sectors in order to assess their attractiveness or otherwise to the investor.

159

○ *Private client stockbrokers*, as the name implies, specialise in dealing with private investors. They will have something to offer for even quite small investors, though it may be in the form of funds rather than shares. They may have a financial services arm, which will deal with other types of investment, including pensions and insurances, and will usually offer PEPs.

Stockbrokers are paid through the dealing commission they charge on the transaction when you buy or sell. They may also make charges for separate services, such as managing your investments. There is now a good deal of competition among brokers for private client custom, and charges vary a lot, so it is well worth shopping around before you decide on a broker.

○ *Sharedealing services* offer the simplest kind of stockbroking service: buying and selling without frills and without advice. Increasingly, you can deal instantly over the phone at very little cost if you are prepared to make your own decisions.

There are three main types of service offered by stockbrokers: discretionary, advisory, and execution-only.

DISCRETIONARY

The discretionary service is the traditional, top-of-the-range managed service whereby you give the broker 'discretion' over your portfolio. In other words, you hand over the power to manage it, the broker buying and selling holdings as he or she thinks fit. The broker won't ask your views prior to dealing, though he or she will let you know about changes to your portfolio once the deal has been done.

The service is for those who haven't the time, or the expertise, for investment questions, and want to leave the job to someone else. Of course, you can give general instructions about what to buy.

You may wish to have a high-income portfolio, or you may be looking for capital growth only. Perhaps you prefer to avoid investing in certain markets or certain types of company – arms or tobacco concerns, for example. All these instructions can be built into your portfolio, which will be tailored to your needs.

Q&A

Q *How does a discretionary broker get access to my money. Isn't it dangerous, handing your money over to someone else?*

A When your assets are under discretionary management they will be held in the broker's nominee company so that the broker has free access to them in order to buy and sell. There are various safeguards covering nominee arrangements (see page 174).

Q *So when my money is in a discretionary account I can just forget all about it?*

A You should not just ignore your investments, even if they are being managed for you on a discretionary basis. Since stockbrokers make money partly through commissions on individual deals, frequent buying and selling is in their interest. This is known as 'churning': dealing to generate commissions rather than because it is good for the portfolio. Churning should be less common under the stringent requirements of the Financial Services Act, and should not occur if your assets are managed by a reputable and conscientious broker.

Q *How much will a stockbroker's services cost?*

A Stockbrokers' charges are complicated, and may vary depending on the nature of the portfolio and the work required. There are usually two main figures to look for with discretionary management: the annual management charge and the rate of commission on dealing.

Annual management is usually quoted as a percentage, with a minimum figure attached. A broker aiming to offer a de luxe service to larger clients might quote 1% on the first £250,000 with a minimum of £1,250 a year. The percentage charge could be as low as 0·3 to 0·4%, with a £200 or £300 annual minimum.

There will usually be dealing commissions on top of this, and they can range widely. Commissions of 0·85% up to 1·25% are typical, though if the annual charge is high one would expect commission to be relatively low.

Some brokers do not charge an annual management fee, but deal on commission only. They may quote a higher commission rate – perhaps 1·6% or more – and may also charge separately for items like valuations. They are more likely to be catering for smaller investors.

Q *What is the minimum investment for discretionary management in shares?*

A Stockbrokers rarely quote a specific minimum sum which they are prepared to accept for discretionary portfolio management, but their charges will suggest the minimum viable amount they aim to stick to. For a discretionary portfolio, most would expect a minimum of at least £50,000, and probably more.

ADVISORY

Many investors nowadays want to take part in the decisions relating to their own portfolios, rather than leaving it all to the broker. If this is what you want, you should go for an advisory service.

With this arrangement the stockbroker will contact you periodically to suggest portfolio changes, but you have the final say on whether to deal or not. This has the advantage over the discretionary portfolio that your stockbroker will automatically be in contact with some frequency, and you will have a chance to chat about your needs and the opportunities available. It might be difficult to operate through an advisory service if you are often away from home.

Q&A

Q *And the cost?*

A Charges for an advisory service are structured in a way that is broadly similar to those on discretionary portfolios. Some stockbrokers charge more for the advisory service than for discretionary management, because there is extra work involved in contacting you every time they want to recommend a deal. Some charge more for discretionary management, because it is the most comprehensive service, and they are taking on greater responsibility for your assets. A few brokers make no distinction between the two services.

Q *What formalities are involved?*

A Any type of service which includes advice on your investment involves a 'fact-find'. This means that you have to fill in a fairly long form giving details of your finances. Your adviser is obliged by the Financial Services Act to take down your details, to make sure he or she is able to offer you something which suits your financial circumstances.

EXECUTION-ONLY

This rather alarming title simply means that the service on offer is dealing only, and has no advice attached. This is obviously meant

Independent financial adviser and *Moneywise* Ask the Professionals panellist Brian Dennehy says:

"Execution-only services can actually be used by investors at two ends of the spectrum: those who trade regularly and know what they're doing, and those who have a portfolio where they're unlikely to make many trades."

for the type of investor who just wants to make his or her own buying and selling decisions.

Execution-only services will vary. Some may offer different levels of administrative help (for instance, a summary of your investments for tax purposes) and some may offer a lot of information on stockmarket companies in order to help you make your own decisions. They may answer questions over the phone, if it is merely a matter of information – for example: What is the yield on this stock? What have been its highs and lows over the last year, and when were they reached? – but they cannot give advice. A typical execution-only investor may be:

- an active investor who buys and sells regularly.
- an investor who has a static portfolio and deals occasionally.
- an investor with one or two privatisation holdings who wants to sell them and realise the cash.

Q&A

Q What about charges?

A There is a lot of competition surrounding execution-only rates. There is no annual fee on this sort of service, which is charged on the basis of dealing commission alone, usually with a stated minimum fee. For example, the charge might be 1% on the first £5,000, with a minimum of £20. A £5,000 bargain could cost anything from £50 to £90, depending on the broker.

Q How do I find an execution-only broker?

A The *APCIMS Directory* (see Directory, page 189) lists member brokers who offer such a service. Brokers also advertise this kind of service locally and in the financial press.

Q Are there lots of formalities with this type of service as well?

A No. Execution-only accounts can be opened with very little effort, and once opened will allow you to deal in bargain sizes of several thousand pounds. At least one stockbroker attached to a major bank will allow you to buy up to £7,500 of stock immediately, once you have given your postcode as an identity check.

OTHER SERVICES FROM STOCKBROKERS

In addition to buying, selling and advising on shares, stockbrokers will invest on your behalf in gilts and other bonds. They may also offer unit trusts or investments trusts. There may be pension specialists within the firm, and some stockbrokers have particular expertise in futures and options or in smaller companies investment. Some brokers offer a full financial planning service, including insurance and other needs as well as stockmarket investment.

When you need a stockbroker

HOW DO YOU KNOW if you need a stockbroker? The key element is the need to buy or sell shares. You may or may not have a large sum of money to invest. You may or may not need advice on how to invest it.

What will your reception be when you approach a stockbroker? Some will be happy to do a very small execution-only deal for you. Others will say your portfolio of £100,000 isn't large enough for their discretionary service. The trick, therefore, is to find the right stockbroker for you.

Stockbroking is traditionally a personal service, and stockbrokers will usually be willing to talk to you and to give one-off help without asking you to make a commitment. The introductory meeting is free.

Stockbrokers, unlike insurance advisers, do not make a fat commission from selling individual products, and are therefore probably more likely to tell you straight away if they are unable to help you, rather than trying to sell you a policy whether or not it is

EXAMPLE
Say you inherit £80,000 from your late mother and are waiting for the money to come through. You are interested in the stockmarket and think that some, at least, of the portfolio will go into shares. You visit a local stockbroker who has an office in the high street. To avoid any delay once your money actually comes through, you can set up an account in advance, so you can deal without further formality once you actually receive the money.

suitable. However, if insurance forms part of your financial needs, stockbrokers increasingly have financial services departments which can help clients in this area too.

HOW TO CHOOSE A STOCKBROKER

The free *APCIMS Directory* (see Directory, page 189) is the best place to start. The Association of Private Client Stockbrokers and Investment Managers represents 85 stockbrokers with branches all over the British Isles. Many of its members encourage business from the smaller investor (the directory lists those which do).

Choose three or four from the firms listed with branches in your area, checking as far as possible that they offer the specialisations you need. You can contact them initially by phone, but you may find it easier to do so by letter so that you can make exactly the same approach to each, and see how they respond. Explain to each broker what you want, and say something about your financial situation (see the sample letter, page 166). Ask for an indication of how each broker would approach your case.

Study the replies to eliminate those which are clearly not suitable, and hold a 'beauty parade' of the remainder: visit them and have a chat (see 'Points to remember', page 166). Having held your beauty parade, hopefully a clear choice will emerge.

Your chosen broker will ask you to sign a client agreement letter. This may be only two sides of an A4 sheet, or it may run to fifteen pages. It will include a detailed financial information form for you to fill in. This will cover the broker's terms and conditions, including everything from charges and how to terminate your relationship to the risk levels involved in derivatives trading.

You will need to decide whether you want to choose an advisory or a discretionary account. The flowchart on page 23 will help.

If you want to remain involved in running your portfolio, with regular valuations, bulletins and advice from the broker, then choose advisory. If you are not interested in the stockmarket or are too busy, discretionary management might suit you better.

Sample letter

Dear stockbroker,

I am writing to enquire about your services as I am considering appointing a stockbroker to manage my assets.

I am 42 and married with two children aged 15 and 10. On the death of my mother I inherited her house and other assets, worth around £150,000 in total. My husband is employed as a systems manager, and his income is adequate for our needs. I therefore wish to invest my inheritance for the future. Specific needs might be additional funding for retirement and university costs for my children. I earn approximately £12,000 a year from supply teaching and would, of course, like to keep my tax liability to a minimum.

I would be grateful if you would let me have details of your services, together with some general comments on the investments you would regard as appropriate for my portfolio.

Yours sincerely,

Mrs A Client

Usually the broker will ask you for a deposit before you begin to trade. For a £50,000 investment you might be asked for a £10,000 deposit, with the balance being payable on settlement day. Penal rates of interest are charged to clients who do not settle on time. With stockmarket settlement cycles now very short (see page 172), clients tend more and more to deposit their cash with their broker, or authorise him or her to debit their bank account directly.

POINTS TO REMEMBER

○ Am I speaking to the person who would handle my account?

○ Do I like and trust that person? Are they easy to talk to?

○ Do they seem to know what they're talking about? Do they have special expertise?

○ Are they ready to take time to deal with me, or are they in a hurry to get rid of me?

○ Will my account be given importance, or will I be a very small fish in a big fund management operation?

○ Are they realistic about the growth prospects on my portfolio? Are they taking care to remind me of the risks involved in stockmarket investment or are they promising the moon?

Choosing a stockbroker: your step-by-step guide

1 Get the *APCIMS Directory* and choose a number of suitable candidates.

2 Write to them, outlining your needs and financial situation.

3 Depending on the answers, choose two or three to speak to in detail.

4 On the basis of your beauty parade, choose the broker for you.

5 Fill in the client agreement form and make the necessary banking arrangements.

6 Hand over your portfolio for discretionary management, or get ready to make your own decisions.

○ Do they have the special expertise to deal with my particular interests, such as pensions?
○ Have they explained their charges to me in full?
○ How do they treat unit trust commissions? Do they take commission, or is some of it rebated?
○ How often will I get a statement of my portfolio, or other communications?
○ Will they provide tax summaries of my investments at year-end?
○ Is their suggested service and recommended portfolio really in line with what I want, or are they pushing me towards a standard service for their own convenience?

How to buy and sell shares

STOCKBROKERS USED TO MOVE about the floor of the Stock Exchange buying and selling person-to-person. Nowadays, share dealings are all done by machine in the UK.

This is what happens in a typical share deal:

1 You phone your broker at stockbrokers ABC at 3.27 pm and ask him to buy 1,000 Glaxo shares.

2 He taps in the Glaxo code and gets prices up on his screen. He

Could a stockbroker help you?

See if your circumstances match one of the examples shown below.

YOU ARE 50-PLUS Maturing life policies, savings and inherited cash give you £60,000. You want to invest it for growth, and to boost savings in retirement.
Comment: Though you have substantial savings you are still a relatively small client for a stockbroker. However, many stockbrokers will be happy to take you on. Assuming you can tolerate the risk, some might be prepared to invest your money in equities. Others might advise you to spread the risk by using unit trusts or investment trusts.

YOU ARE IN YOUR 40S AND SELF-EMPLOYED You have several pension policies amounting to £80,000 in value and would like to draw them together and get advice on the spread of funds.

Comment: With £80,000 you could consider a self-invested personal pension, which would achieve your aims. Some stockbrokers offer these – but be sure they have experience in the pensions area before committing yourself.

YOU ARE RETIRED AND HAVE £20,000 IN THE BUILDING SOCIETY You urgently need extra income.
Comment: You are a small client, but many stockbrokers will be willing to help, and can advise on a good, low-risk return through fixed-interest investments.

YOU HAVE PRIVATISATION HOLDINGS AMOUNTING TO £5,000 You don't know whether to hold them or cash them in.
Comment: Drop in to a local branch of a private client stockbroker and ask advice. Look out for stockbrokers offering special dealing discounts.

looks to see which market maker is offering the best price (or 'strip price'). Let's call them XYZ.

3   Your broker rings XYZ and asks for a quote on Glaxo. The conversation is as follows:

Broker: ABC, 333. Glaxo, please.
XYZ market maker: Eight ten fifteen.
Broker: Have you anything inside that?
Market maker: OK, eight ten fourteen.
Broker: That suits. I'm a buyer of 1,000 shares at fourteen.
Market maker: Sold 1,000 at 14. 777. Time 15.30.

This conversation needs a translation to the uninitiated. After announcing the name of his firm and its identifying code, or 'counterparty code', your broker asks XYZ to quote a price on Glaxo. He does not say whether he wants to buy or sell.

Could a stockbroker help you? continued

YOU WANT TO SET UP A SELF-SELECT PEP
so you can choose your own investments, but are not quite confident you
could manage on your own.
Comment: Many stockbrokers offer self-
select PEPs at low cost. Some also offer
advice when you need it as part of the
service.

YOU HAVE £10,000 IN SAVINGS plus
£100 a month which you want to invest
for balanced growth.
Comment: A broker who welcomes
smaller clients would take you on, but
probably through unit trusts. It isn't
practical to deal directly in shares on
£100 a month.

**YOU HAVE £2,500 WHICH YOU WANT TO
USE FOR A FLUTTER** on the stockmarket,
but you don't know where to start.
Comment: If you really have no idea, a
stockbroker will probably suggest that
you buy a general unit trust until you
have built up a little more money and
experience. If you have some ideas, but
need a little help, ask for one-off advice.
If you are likely to have regular sums to
invest, it would be worth becoming an
advisory client.

**YOUR RECENTLY WIDOWED MOTHER HAS
£150,000** from the sale of her home.
She does not need income now, but
may later on. She wants tax-efficient
growth, perhaps with provisions for
future nursing home fees. She doesn't
want to worry about her portfolio.
Comment: Many stockbrokers would
welcome your mother as a client.
They handle needs like hers all the
time. Make sure she chooses a broker
who is efficient and whom she gets
on with.

The XYZ dealer tells him he is trading in Glaxo at 810p to 815p (buying and selling prices). Your broker tries to get a better price, still without saying whether he wants to sell or buy. XYZ offers 810p to 814p. This is what the man from ABC was looking for. He puts in his buy order. The dealer confirms the order and gives his own counterparty code and agrees the time of the deal.

Had the dealer said "eight eleven fifteen" – in other words, raising the price at which he was prepared to buy, rather than reducing the price at which he would sell – your broker might have said "That doesn't suit, I'll try on", and called another market maker.

4 When they put the phone down, both broker and market maker key details of the deal they have done into the SEAQ

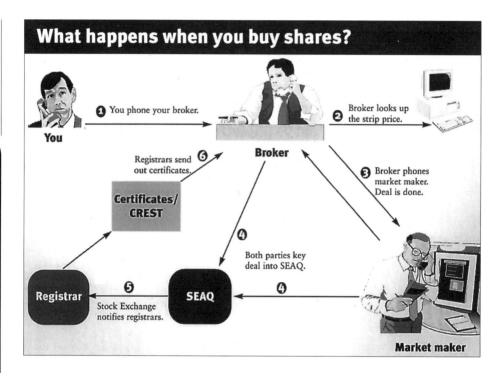

What happens when you buy shares?

You — ① You phone your broker.

Broker — ② Broker looks up the strip price.

③ Broker phones market maker. Deal is done.

Registrars send out certificates. ⑥

Certificates/CREST

④ Both parties key deal into SEAQ.

Registrar — ⑤ Stock Exchange notifies registrars. **SEAQ** ④

Market maker

system on their own computers. SEAQ is the Stock Exchange Automated Quotation System, the on-line system used by all brokers and market makers. At the end of the day, both sides of the bargain made by the two counterparties should balance.

5 The Stock Exchange notifies the Glaxo registrars that you have bought the shares.

6 After some weeks the registrars will send you a share certificate. If you are dealing through the ABC nominee company, the certificates will go to ABC. Since the arrival of CREST transactions are increasingly done electronically, without the need for physical certificates.

PAPERWORK

When you deal with a stockbroker, you can expect to receive a certain amount of documentation. Nowadays there is a lot of emphasis on disclosure of charges and on making forms and brochures easy to read – but you may still find there are things you don't understand.

When you decide to buy or sell your shares you will get a copy

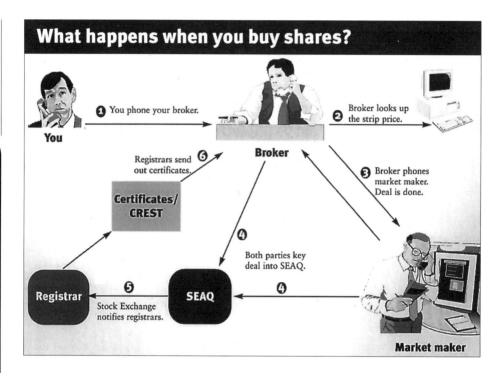

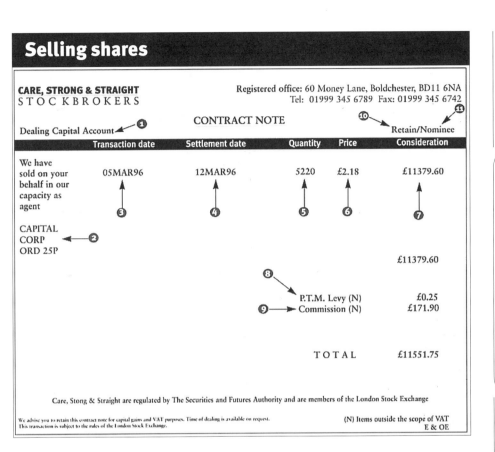

Selling shares

CARE, STRONG & STRAIGHT
S T O C K B R O K E R S

Registered office: 60 Money Lane, Boldchester, BD11 6NA
Tel: 01999 345 6789 Fax: 01999 345 6742

CONTRACT NOTE

Dealing Capital Account ← ❶   Retain/Nominee ❿ ⓫

	Transaction date	Settlement date	Quantity	Price	Consideration
We have sold on your behalf in our capacity as agent	05MAR96 ❸	12MAR96 ❹	5220 ❺	£2.18 ❻	£11379.60 ❼
CAPITAL CORP ← ❷ ORD 25P					
					£11379.60
❽			P.T.M. Levy (N)		£0.25
❾ →			Commission (N)		£171.90
			T O T A L		£11551.75

Care, Stong & Straight are regulated by The Securities and Futures Authority and are members of the London Stock Exchange

We advise you to retain this contract note for capital gains and VAT purposes. Time of dealing is available on request.
This transaction is subject to the rules of the London Stock Exchange.

(N) Items outside the scope of VAT
E & OE

STOCKBROKER SERVICES

of a contract note, giving the exact details of the bargain. The illustration above shows an example, where the investor has sold shares in Capital Corporation.

Key:

1 Type of account – the name which the broker gives to its standard, taxable dealing account. Alternatives might be a PEP or pension account.
2 Name of security being bought.
3 Date on which the bargain was done. If the share price moved a lot on that day, and the investor wants to check the precise time, the broker will tell him.
4 Day by which payment is due on the bargain.
5 Number of shares sold.
6 Selling price per share. Some share prices are shown as fractions – in 8ths, 16ths, 32nds or 64ths. Others are shown in decimals.

This simply depends on the way they are quoted in the market.

7 Total price to be received for the shares.

8 Panel of Takeovers & Mergers Levy – a flat charge on large share bargains which helps fund the PTM. If the investor had been buying, not selling, the contract note would look very similar except that this item would be replaced by the transfer stamp – another name for stamp duty, which is a 0·5% tax on all share purchases.

9 Stockbroker's commission – what the stockbroker charges for doing the deal.

10 Shows whether the proceeds should be kept within the broker's deposit account to earn interest on the client's behalf, or paid out to the client. If proceeds were to be paid out this item would say 'pay away' and the client would receive a cheque five days after dealing.

11 Shows the shares are held in the broker's nominee account, rather than being held by the investor personally.

HOW TO PAY UP

If you are new to the stockmarket, there is a certain amount to learn about when and how you pay for your share purchases. Payment systems, like everything else on the stockmarket, have changed radically in the last few years after many years of dealing under an arrangement of fixed fortnightly 'settlement days'.

The new system is known as rolling settlement. It gives the investor a specified number of days in which to pay for a share purchase. The period is currently five days. The market aims to move to a system of three-day settlement, though in mid-1997 a date for this had not yet been fixed.

As the settlement period gets shorter, the market also aims to move to paperless trading, outlawing share certificates – the traditional means of confirming your ownership of shares. The idea is to make administration a lot easier for both large and small investors. However, many private investors still prefer to have a piece of paper which confirms their shareholding, and it will probably be some years before share certificates disappear altogether.

In order to make paperless dealing possible a new dealing system, CREST, was introduced in summer 1996. CREST is an electronic means of holding shares and recording share ownership – just as your money is largely held not in notes and coins but as a computer record at the bank. CREST effectively does away with the need for share certificates, and means that share transactions can be put through the computer system automatically, making them faster and less liable to error. It should also result in lower transaction costs and more rapid availability of information, and shares you have bought will be legally recorded as belonging to you much more quickly. Whereas share certificates can take some weeks to come through, the registrar will register a CREST transfer within two hours.

Private investors can take advantage of CREST by:

○ holding shares through the nominee service offered by a broker who is a CREST member.
○ becoming a sponsored member of CREST.

Sponsored membership means the individual is a named member, but still carries out all dealings through a sponsor – the broker. Sponsored membership is likely to appeal only to larger, more active investors.

There is no obligation for investors to join CREST. They can go on buying and selling shares in the traditional way, signing a transfer form and passing the certificates to the broker in order to sell, and receiving new certificates when shares are bought. Investors who deal in this way will probably need a longer settlement period than five days.

Whether the old system will remain viable remains to be seen. It is possible that stockbrokers will eventually begin to encourage smaller investors into the CREST system by increasing charges on traditional paper dealing.

Q&A

Q If I deal within CREST, can I get out?

A Yes, if you are dealing within the CREST system it will still be possible to get your holdings out in the form of share certificates.

Q How can I keep track of my holdings without any share certificates?

A Whatever kind of stockbroker service you use, you will still receive contract notes every time you buy and sell, and you can use these to keep records of your holdings.

NOMINEE ACCOUNTS: IS THERE A CHOICE?

For many private investors – those who do not trade often enough to be sponsored members, but who want their dealings to be within the electronic system – it will be necessary to use a CREST member's (ie your broker's) nominee service.

A nominee service is an arrangement whereby your broker, or rather its associated nominee company, holds your investments on your behalf. You hand over your share certificates to the nominee company. You will then have no need to post the certificates to your broker when you sell shares.

Some private investors are wary of nominee services because it means handing over your certificates to the nominee company. But with the move to rolling settlement there is much less time to settle a transaction. Five-day dealing outside a nominee service can only work if you are very efficient and there are no mishaps such as postal delays (see the box below).

This will not work if you give the order and then go off on a business trip, for example, if you have mislaid your share certificates, or if you simply don't get your post until after working hours. Unless you deal only occasionally, a nominee service is the only practical way of coping with dealing for five-day settlement through CREST. Those who don't wish to use the nominee account will have to trade over a ten-day settlement period instead. Most private client brokers will still deal in this way.

Many brokers build a nominee service into portfolio management or dealing arrangements without extra charge. Some make a separate charge for the use of a nominee account. There may also be a number of add-on services, some of which may attract an extra charge. These might include:

O sending annual reports and accounts

Independent financial adviser and *Moneywise* Ask the Professionals panellist Brian Dennehy says:

"Moving to such short settlement periods means that pretty well everyone will have to hold shares in nominee accounts, because you won't be able to settle in time using the post. Ultimately I suspect a vast proportion of individual investors' dealing will be done on the Internet."

FIVE-DAY SETTLEMENT
MONDAY: you instruct your broker to buy some stock. The broker does so and posts you the sale contract note.
TUESDAY: you get the contract note. You write a cheque and send it by return of post.
WEDNESDAY: your broker gets the cheque. It takes three days to clear which takes until ...
MONDAY: the due date for settlement.

EXAMPLE

EXAMPLE
A client who has been with a broker for several years decides to switch to the nominee service when five-day settlement is introduced. She finds that the broker intends to charge £20 for each report and accounts she wants to receive. She has in the past received reports and accounts, but never looks at them, so opts not to get them in the future. Her friend, who has been with the same broker for even longer, is an avid amateur share-picker. She likes to get any company information which is going. When she hears about the new charge, she decides not to use the nominee service.

○ passing on the right to attend AGMs
○ informing investors of scrip issues
○ passing on shareholder perks
○ paying out dividends

It is hard to generalise about nominee service charges. The only thing you can do is choose which services are important to you, and compare the charges from two or three brokers offering the features you want. Dealing costs on a £10,000 bargain might range from £10 to £150 or more, sometimes including the nominee service and sometimes not.

Though your assets are kept account of within the nominee account, the nominee itself is counted as a single investor. For this reason, some companies refuse to give voting rights and shareholder perks to investors holding shares through the nominee. The private investor organisation Proshare has developed a Nominee Code which it hopes issuing companies will adhere to, and which should remove voting and perks problems for nominee investors.

Q&A

Q How can I be sure my broker's nominee account is safe?

A A nominee company is an independently run subsidiary of your broker. There is no special regulator to cover nominees, but the parent company will be regulated and would accept responsibility in the event of loss. As nominees have become more important, brokers have laid emphasis on their financial strength or that of their parent group, and on the indemnity insurance they offer. This may run to several million pounds per client in the event of loss through error or fraud.

Q What if my shares get confused with someone else's in the nominee?

A Find out whether your broker's nominee is 'pooled' or 'designated'. Pooled accounts merge all holdings. Designated accounts have your name attached to your investments in the nominee.

Q But won't I still have to send a cheque to pay for purchases?

A Nominee services often have a bank account attached. This way, your broker can pay the proceeds of a sale directly into a bank account in your name, and if you want to buy he can draw on your account to get payment. Dividends can be paid into the bank account and most brokers pay a competitive rate of interest.

Q What if I don't join the nominee service?

A Most brokers will still accept non-nominee dealing, though doubts have been raised in the industry about how long this can continue. As to cost, there is some disagreement. Some brokers charge non-nominee clients more, some the same as, and some less than those who use the nominee service. Share prices are still the same however you deal, but now SETS has come into use (see page 31) they could increase for those who continue to hold certificates.

DEALING BY POST OR PHONE

Investors who own shares in two or three privatisation issues only, and who may want at some point to sell their shares and realise the cash, do not need a full discretionary or advisory service.

Postal sharedealing, which has become popular in recent years, is designed for this kind of investor, who has limited needs, wants to deal cheaply, and does not expect to have the share price confirmed at the time the deal is done. Postal dealing may also be of use to those who hold shares through an employee share purchase scheme.

Postal dealing is offered particularly by execution-only brokers and building society broking services. These services allow you to sell (not buy) at low cost and without a face-to-face visit to a stockbroker. Though intended primarily for small lots of shares, holdings up to quite a high limit (say £20,000) may be accepted. Your cheque is posted back to you, usually on the settlement day.

Postal services are mostly limited to the privatisation issues or maybe a list of the most widely held shares, though at least one service covers all quoted shares.

With most postal services you need to become a member for a small joining fee. You must provide information which can be used as identification, though this can be done quite easily over the phone.

Costs vary substantially, so it is worth shopping around. For a £2,500 bargain you might pay as little as £15 or less, or up to £40

Do you need a nominee account?

Do you want to go on holding share certificates?

↓

Do you deal often (more than 2–3 times a year), or are you often away from home?

Yes → to either/both

No → to both

If neither applies, does your stockbroker offer acceptable terms for paper-based dealing?

Yes ↓   **No** →

Shop around to find a broker whose terms suit you better.

Are you happy to accept the paperwork and security aspects of holding your own certificates?

No ←   **Yes** ↓

Are you prepared to pay more for paper dealing in the future?

Yes ↓   **No** ↓

Would you be prepared to switch to a nominee service?

↓

Does your stockbroker offer acceptable nominee terms?

No ↓   **Yes** ↓

Do you receive shareholder perks from any of the 'problem' stocks (see Chapter 4)?

Yes ↓   **No** ↓

These stocks will have to be held in certified form form to continue getting perks.

If you buy any such stocks you will not be able to get the perks if you hold through nominees.

A nominee service might be most suitable for you.

You are dedicated to paper dealing! You may wish to think again if costs are weighted against you in the future.

Monitor the situation and consider a nominee service in the future.

Do you deal frequently (2–3 times a year or more), travel often, dislike paperwork, prefer not to hold valuable documents or want a five-day settlement of bargains?
If yes, to any or all of these, a nominee service is right for you.

or more through the dearer services. Most services offer a family package deal, with a special price for all family members at the same address.

If you want to deal with few formalities but on a more regular basis you might want to consider a telephone dealing service, which will offer additional features like nominee accounts and share price and company information. It may even offer a deposit account through which you can channel cash for your share dealings.

Phone services are offered by high street banks and building societies, but if you are interested look at what is on offer from local stockbrokers as well. They may have more facilities and a more personal approach for little or no extra cost.

If you want to sell shares and invest in less risky investment funds you can take your shares directly to a fund management company offering a share exchange scheme (see Chapter 5).

How to complain

LIKE ANY OTHER KIND of financial adviser, stockbrokers are regulated under the Financial Services Act.

STEP-BY-STEP GUIDE ON HOW TO COMPLAIN

1 Take your problem to a senior representative of the firm, as soon as possible after it occurs. The firm has to deal promptly with your complaint.
2 Still not satisfied? Go to the the Securities and Futures Authority (SFA) Complaints Bureau. The SFA is the regulator responsible for stockbrokers. The Complaints Bureau looks into complaints and tries to conciliate.

EXAMPLE
An investor has two privatisation holdings, and is left another on the death of a relative. The holdings total £10,000 in value. He decides to realise the investment, but wants the best possible price for the shares.

He enquires about a postal dealing service and finds he can have a say over the price at which he sells by opting for the price limit feature. With this type of arrangement, for which there will be a charge, you can state the minimum price at which you are prepared to sell.

The broker will hold onto your share certificates for an agreed term until that price is reached or the term expires. One or two services will hold your certificates for up to a year on this basis, again for a small extra charge.

The investor sets prices on his holdings. The market is buoyant, and they are all sold within a month.

3 Still no solution? You can now take your case to the SFA Consumer Arbitration Scheme. There is a £50 charge and claims up to £50,000 can be accepted. If you choose to go to arbitration, you cannot subsequently sue the firm.

4 If the Arbitration Panel decides against the firm, it can order the broker to pay compensation in cash or stock. If it finds against you, you can appeal to the Arbitration Appeals Panel.

5 If you are still dissatisfied, you can take your case to the independent Complaints Commissioner, who can look at how the case has been handled (not at the case itself). He can pass it back to the SFA to be looked at again.

The SFA will consider cases which:

○ relate to SFA business

○ are not already under litigation or arbitration and where

○ the relevant events happened on or after 29th April 1988 (when the Financial Services Act came into force).

If your stockbroker goes bust, investments held in the nominee company should be safe but bargains still going through the system could be affected. If you lost money in this way you could approach the Investors Compensation Scheme, which has a compensation limit of £48,000. The SFA will be incorporated into the new overall regulator – the Financial Services Authority – due to take over responsibility in 1999.

Action plan

○ Decide if you need a stockbroker.

○ If you have limited holdings you wish to sell (such as privatisation issues), consider a postal service.

○ For simple execution-only dealing, consider a telephone service.

○ Talk to several stockbrokers, compare what they offer, and make your choice.

○ Having chosen a broker, be prepared to spend some time discussing your needs and choosing the right kind of service for you.

○ Decide whether to use the broker's nominee service or stick with share certificates (see page 177).

○ Once you are an established client, continue to take an interest in your investments to make sure they are performing in accordance with your requirements.

10 Looking after your investments

The business of understanding and choosing stockmarket investments is complicated. But looking after them once you have made your choice is a lot easier.

Keeping records

IF YOU ARE RUNNING your own affairs without using a stockbroker's nominee company you will need to keep track of the papers generated by your investments.

❍ Keep all contract notes filed in date order. This will provide a complete record of your portfolio for your own monitoring purposes and for calculating capital gains tax. Check that the details are correct on each contract note as you receive it.

❍ Keep full details of all dividends received and file tax credits together to be submitted with your tax return.

❍ If you still hold your own share certificates, they should be kept in a safe but accessible place – you will need to be able to get hold of them easily in case you want to sell.

❍ You will need some way of monitoring the progress of your investments. This could be in the form of a handwritten chart listing the name and quantity of the investments held, the purchase price, the value at succeeding valuation dates, and perhaps the percentage change compared to the last valuation.

This level of information will give you a basic monitoring system which will be perfectly adequate if you have only a few investments to keep track of. If you have a large portfolio or want a more sophisticated approach, there are a number of software packages on the market which will allow you to update valuations and graph out your portfolio's performance on a PC screen.

○ If your affairs are at all complicated you may be better off using a stockbroker's nominee company, or relying on a management service. Your stockbroker will provide regular statements and tax breakdowns which can be handed to your accountant.

Tax

SURPRISINGLY, PERHAPS, the tax levied on stockmarket returns is quite simple to understand. Income tax is paid on dividends, and capital gains tax on any taxable gains. If your investment is made through a PEP, it is completely free of both taxes and need not be declared on your tax return.

INCOME TAX

Share dividends are paid out net of tax at 20%. The dividend cheque is accompanied by a tax voucher, which shows the amount of the dividend and the tax already paid on your behalf by the company to the Inland Revenue. The tax already paid is called a tax credit.

It is important to keep tax credit slips, either to prove to the Inland Revenue the amount of income you have received, or the amount you want to reclaim if you are a non-taxpayer. If you are a higher-rate taxpayer you will have to pay the difference between the tax credit and the amount owing.

CAPITAL GAINS TAX

Capital gains tax (CGT) is due on all types of stockmarket investment except gilts, which are exempt. There is an annual exemption on gains up to a certain amount (£6,500 in 1997/98), and gains are also indexed. In other words, the purchase price is raised to take account of inflation before the gain is calculated (indexation only applies to gains since 30th March 1982). CGT is hard to work out. Leave it to an accountant if your investment portfolio is very active.

Because of indexation and the exempt limit, you have to make considerable gains before you run up a CGT bill. Even then you can reduce your potential liability by a strategy known as 'bed and breakfasting'. This entails selling your shares one day and buying them back the next. By doing this before you actually have a CGT liability, you 'rebase' the purchase cost of your investment and set the CGT clock back to zero.

Bed and breakfasting is a common transaction, and stockbrokers and fund management groups often give special delaying terms. But there will be some cost involved and in addition your money will be at risk overnight. If the price of your shares rises between the two transactions you may have to put more money in or settle for a reduced holding.

The calculations are relatively straightforward if you are looking at a single investment which you have bought and sold. But the position is not quite so easy where you have a whole series of shares in the same company or units in the same trust which you have bought at different times – how do you decide which shares or units you sold? There are special rules for this.

Shares and units are pooled and treated as disposed of in the following order:

❍ Shares or units bought on the same day as the sale (or other disposal).

❍ Shares or units bought up to ten days before the sale.

❍ Shares or units acquired on or after 6th April 1982.

❍ Shares or units acquired between 6th April 1965 and 5th April 1982.

❍ Shares or units acquired before 6th April 1965 (unless you pool these with the 1965–82 shares).

Where shares are lumped together in one of these groups, you match your sale to the most recently acquired shares first and work backwards.

A special concession applies to unit trusts and investment trusts if you are investing through a monthly scheme. Strictly speaking, each monthly payment is a different investment.

Independent financial adviser and *Moneywise* Ask the Professionals panellist Rebekah Kearey says:

"There are two potential pitfalls with bed and breakfast activity. The first is the movement of prices. If the value of the asset increases dramatically overnight, you buy it back at a higher price and lose out. Of course, if it drops overnight you gain. The other danger is the cost of sale and repurchase. The potential tax saving must outweigh the charges that could be incurred to sell and repurchase or no saving is made."

To reduce the calculations, you can ask to be allowed to add together all your payments for the trust's accounting year and (after deducting minor withdrawals) have them treated as a single investment made in the seventh month. Distributions which are reinvested are also to be scooped up into this simplified calculation.

If you have shares received as a result of a rights issue or bonus issue, these belong to the same pool as the original shares they were based on. When you sell rights issue shares, you take the cost of the original shares plus the cost of the rights issue shares. You deduct the relevant indexation allowance from each. Add the result together and divide by the total number of shares. Then multiply the result by the number of shares you sold.

Bonus shares are free, but this will still affect the cost. If you buy 2,000 share for £4,000 and then receive 500 bonus shares, the cost per share for CGT purposes falls from £2 to £1·60.

Information

THE PRIVATE INVESTOR who wants to do his or her own research has a mass of sources to choose from. The Proshare Guide to Information Sources for the Private Investor gives a very comprehensive list.

○ The press offers a wide range of material, ranging from pricing information and features on individual companies to sector analyses and articles on investment strategy.
○ Tipsheets usually have quite high subscription costs, but give concrete suggestions on what to buy.
○ The broadcast media has a range of coverage, and TV Text pages give free real-time prices and financial news in brief.
○ There are a number of information services with widely varying subscription prices available by post, by phone, by a PC link-up or even through the use of pagers. These services may offer market-wide information, or details of individual named companies.
○ PC software packages help you analyse data in conjunction with your own portfolio, graphing out performance in a number of different ways. Most have a link with a price updating service which feeds information straight into your computer. Prices vary a lot. Obviously you will need to check that:

• You have adequate hardware to run the package.

• The software is up-to-date and easy to use.

• The package contains all the features you are likely to need without having to buy expensive add-ons.

• You are not paying a fortune for features you will never use.

○ Now that the Internet is becoming more widely used, access to information for private investors has multiplied enormously. Many of the organisations mentioned in the Directory have their own web sites, which in some cases give enormous amounts of data. Paid-for services may give a useful quantity of information free. The companies in which you want to invest may also have their own Internet pages.

○ Finally, don't forget the most basic item of information: the company report. Companies you are interested in will send you a copy of their latest report free. The *Financial Times* offers a free report service for many of the companies listed in its prices pages. Many publications offer a free service to put you in touch with advertisers, which may be a good way to get in contact with managers of stockmarket funds or with specialist advisers.

Action plan

○ Establish a system for keeping records of your stockmarket transactions.

○ Make sure that you're clear about the tax implications of your investment activity.

○ Investigate reliable sources of information and keep a look-out for any potential new sources.

An A-Z guide to financial words and phrases

Accrual rate The rate at which pension entitlement builds up. Often expressed as a fraction of your final salary for each year served, for example 1/60, 1/80. Can be used to refer to Inland Revenue limits on how a pension entitlement builds up. Also can refer to the actual pension entitlement built up for each year of membership of a final salary company pension scheme.

Additional voluntary contributions (AVCs) Extra payments paid into company pension schemes by members to improve their benefits.

Annual percentage rate (APR) The real cost, in terms of interest and fees, of credit (used for comparison purposes).

Annuity A form of income bought through insurance companies with the proceeds from a pension fund, which pays a guaranteed sum throughout your lifetime.

Base rate The interest rate set by the Bank of England, used as a basis for the rates that banks offer their customers.

Basic state pension Flat rate pension payable to all individuals who have made sufficient National Insurance contributions.

Bid-to-offer spread The difference between the price at which investments can be bought and the price at which they can then be sold.

Bond A certificate of debt issued by companies and governments to raise cash, usually paying interest and traded in a market.

Capital gains tax (CGT) The tax payable on profits from the sale of assets, particularly shares.

Contracting out A legal arrangement under which you can give up part of your SERPS benefits and build up an equivalent or better benefit in a company scheme or personal pension.

Convertible A security, usually a bond or debenture issued by a company, that can be converted into the ordinary shares or preference shares of that company at a fixed date or dates, and at a fixed price.

Deed of covenant A promise made in a deed, often used as a means of providing funds to charities or to transfer income from one person to another, with a view to saving tax.

Derivative A financial instrument that is valued according to the expected price movements of an underlying asset, for example a share or a currency.

Dividend The distribution of part of the earnings of a company to its shareholders

Earnings per share (EPS) The earnings of a company over a stated period, usually a year, divided by the number of ordinary shares it has issued.

Endowment policy A life insurance and savings policy which pays a specified amount of money on an agreed date, or on the death of the person insured, whichever is sooner.

Equities The ordinary shares of a publicly quoted company.

European Currency Unit (ECU) A form of currency calculated as a weighted average of a basket of EC currencies.

Final salary pension scheme a Company pension scheme in which your pension depends on your salary at retirement, your number of years' service, and the fraction of final salary awarded for each year's service, for example 1/60.

Free-standing additional voluntary contributions (FSAVCs) Extra payments made to boost a pension by investing with an insurance company, not an employer's scheme. See 'AVCs'.

Friendly Society A mutual organisation offering tax-free investment plans with a life-insurance element, normally over ten years.

Fund A reserve of money or investments held for a specific purpose – for example, to be divided into units for investors to buy (as in a unit trust fund) or to provide a pension income (as in a pension fund).

Future A contract to buy or sell a fixed number of commodities, currencies, or shares at a fixed date in the future at a fixed price.

Gearing The ratio of the amount of long-term loans and preference shares to ordinary shares in a company.

Gilt-edged security (gilt) A fixed-interest security issued by the British Government.

Guaranteed income bond (GIB) A bond guaranteeing the full return of capital plus a fixed income, issued by life insurance companies.

Held in trust An arrangement allowing property or cash to be held by a trustee on behalf of a named beneficiary.

Independent financial adviser (IFA) An adviser committed to offering 'best advice' on the range of investments and plans in the marketplace, not someone selling investments from just one company.

Inheritance tax (IHT) A form of wealth tax on inherited money: £215,000 can be inherited before this tax is incurred.

Initial charge The charge paid to the managers of a unit trust by an investor when he or she first buys units – usually between 3% and 5%.

Investment trust A company quoted on the stock exchange which invests in other companies' shares.

Lower earnings limit (LEL) Weekly wage roughly equivalent to the basic state pension. If you earn less than this amount, you do not pay National Insurance contributions. If you earn more that the LEL, your earnings up to the upper earnings limit (UEL) are liable to National Insurance contributions. Earnings between the LEL and the UEL are called middle band earnings.

Middle band earnings Earnings between the lower and upper earnings limits. The SERPS pension relates to these earnings.

Money purchase pension scheme A company pension scheme in which your pension is dependent on the amount paid into the pension fund, and the investment performance of that fund.

Mortgage interest relief at source (MIRAS) Tax relief currently at 15% (10% from April 1998) on the interest on the first £30,000 borrowed to buy a house.

National Insurance contributions Contributions payable on earnings if you earn more than the lower earnings limit, to pay for state benefits and pensions.

Negative equity The condition whereby the current market value of a house is worth less than the amount outstanding on a mortgage.

Net relevant earnings Earnings from self-employment or employment which are used to calculate the maximum payments into a personal pension.

Nominees Individuals or companies which hold shares on behalf of investors, to reduce the costs of administering a portfolio, or to conceal the true owners of the shares.

Offshore funds Funds based outside the UK for tax reasons.

Open market option The right to use a pension fund on retirement to buy an annuity from any insurance company, not just the provider of the pension plan.

Option A contract giving the right (but not the obligation) to buy or sell commodities, currencies or shares at a fixed date in the future at a fixed price.

Pay as you earn (PAYE) The system whereby employers collect tax from employees and pass it on to the Inland Revenue.

Penny shares Securities with a very low market price – investors usually hope for rapid recoveries or takeovers.

Pensionable earnings Earnings on which pension benefits and/or contributions are calculated.

Pensionable service The length of time in a particular job which qualifies for pension benefit. Usually this equates to the length of time as a member of the pension scheme.

Pension transfer A payment made from one pension scheme to another, or to an insurance company running a personal pension scheme to fund a buy-out scheme. Enables pension rights to be moved out of the pension scheme of a previous employer.

Permanent health insurance (PHI) Insurance which replaces income lost due to long-term illness or injury and pays benefits relative to the size of a salary.

Personal allowances Amounts of income which you are allowed tax free.

Personal equity plan (PEP) A plan used to hold UK shares, unit trusts, investment trusts, and now corporate bonds, with any dividends and capital gains free of tax.

Personal pension plan An approved scheme for people who are self-employed or not in a company scheme. Personal pensions are arranged through insurance companies, and are individual money purchase schemes.

Preserved pensions Pension rights built up in a pension scheme, which have been left in that scheme when you ceased employment with that company.

Price/earnings ratio (P/E ratio) The market price of a company share divided by the

earnings per share of that company.

Retail price index (RPI) The official measure of inflation calculated by weighting the costs of goods and services to approximate a typical family spending pattern.

Retirement annuity contract A type of personal pension superseded in 1988 by personal pensions themselves.

Rights issue New shares sold by a company to raise new capital.

Scrip issue The issue of new share certificates to existing shareholders to reflect an accumulation of profits on the balance sheet.

Self-invested personal pension (SIPP) A personal pension under which the member has the ability to control the investments.

Share An investment in and part ownership of a company, conferring the right to part of the company's profits (usually by payment of a dividend), and to any voting rights attached to that share, and which, in the case of public companies, can be traded on the open market.

Split-capital investment trust A limited-life investment trust in which the equity capital is divided into income shares and capital shares.

State earnings-related pension scheme (SERPS) A state pension in addition to the basic state pension, plus widows' benefits and invalidity benefits, based on earnings.

Stockmarket A market for the buying and selling of shares and securities.

Tax-exempt special savings accounts (TESSAs) Five-year savings accounts which are exempt from tax, and available from banks and building societies.

Tax year The tax system works on the basis of tax years which run from 6 April one calendar year to 5 April the next.

Term assurance or insurance Life insurance with no investment element.

Unit-linked policy An insurance policy in which the benefits depend on the performance of units in a fund invested in shares or property.

Unit trust A pooled fund of stockmarket investments divided into equal units.

Upper earnings limit The maximum weekly wage above which there is no liability to National Insurance contributions.

Value-added tax (VAT) A form of indirect taxation borne by traders and consumers, levied on goods and services.

Whole-of-life policy A life insurance policy which pays a specified amount on the death of the life insured.

With-profits policy A life insurance or pension policy with additional amounts added to the sum insured.

Yield The income from an investment.

Zero-rated Goods or services that are taxable for VAT, but with a tax rate of zero.

Directory

REGULATORY BODIES

Investment Managers Regulatory Organisation (IMRO)
Lloyds Chambers, 1 Portsoken Street, London E1 8BT
0171 390 5000

Investors' Compensation Scheme (ICS)
Gavrelle House, 2-14 Bunhill Row, London EC1Y 8RA
0171 638 1240

The Office of the Investment Ombudsman
6 Frederick's Place,
London EC2R 8BT
0171 769 3065

Personal Investment Authority (PIA)
1 Canada Square, Canary Wharf, London E14 5AZ
0171 538 8860

Securities and Futures Authority Ltd (SFA)
Cotton Centre, Cottons Lane,
London SE1 2QB
0171 378 9000

Securities and Investments Board (SIB)
Gavrelle House, 2-14 Bunhill Row, London EC1Y 8RA
0171 638 1240
SIB Central Register (address as above) 0171 929 3652

SAVINGS AND INVESTMENTS

Association of Investment Trust Companies (AITC)
Durrant House, 8-13 Chiswell Street, London EC1Y 4YY
0171 588 5347

Association of Policy Market Makers
Holywell Centre, 1 Phipp Street, London EC2A 4PS
0171 739 3949
(for a list of companies selling second-hand endowments)

Association of Solicitor Investment Managers (ASIM)
Baldocks, Chiddingstone Causeway, Tonbridge, Kent TN11 8JX
01892 870065

Association of Private Client Investment Managers
112 Middlesex Street,
London E1 7HY.
0171 247 7080

Association of Unit Trusts and Investment Funds (AUTIF)
Information Unit, 65 Kingsway, London WC2B 6TD
0171 831 0898

National Savings Information
Room 073, Charles House,
376 Kensington High Street,
London W14 8SD
0645 645000

ProShare
Library Chambers,
13-14 Basinghall Street,
London EC2V 5BQ
0171 600 0984

Stock Exchange
Old Broad Street,
London EC2N 1HP
0171 588 2355

BANKS AND BUILDING SOCIETIES

British Bankers' Association
105-108 Old Broad Street
London EC2N 1EX
0171 216 8800

Banking Ombudsman
70 Grays Inn Road,
London WC1X 8NB
0171 404 9944

Building Societies Association/Council of Mortgage Lenders
3 Savile Row, London W1X 1AF
0171 437 0655

Building Societies Ombudsman
Millbank Tower, Millbank,
London SW1P 4XS
0171 931 0044

PENSIONS

Association of Consulting Actuaries (ACA)
1 Wardrobe Place,
London EC4V 5AH
0171 248 3163

**Occupational Pensions
Advisory Service**
11 Belgrave Road,
London SW1V 1RB
0171 233 8080

Pensions Ombudsman
11 Belgrave Road,
London SW1V 1RB
0171 834 9144

CREDIT REFERENCE AGENCIES

CCN Group Ltd
Consumer Help Service,
PO Box 40,
Nottingham NG7 2SS
0115 986 8172

Equifax Europe Ltd
Consumer Affairs Department,
Spectrum House, 1A North
Avenue, Clydebank,
Glasgow G81 2DR
0141 951 1253

FINANCIAL ADVICE

**Independent Financial Advice
Promotion (IFAP)**
4th Floor, 28 Greville Street,
London EC1N 8SU
0117 971 1177
(for a list of three independent
advisers in your area)

Institute of Financial Planning
Whitefriars Centre,
Lewins Mead,
Bristol BS1 2NT
0117 930 4434

TAX AND ACCOUNTANCY

Adjudicator's Office,
3rd Floor,
Haymarket House,
28 Haymarket,
London SW1Y 4SP.
0171 930 2292

Capital Taxes Office
Ferrers House
PO Box 38,
Castle Meadow Road,
Nottingham NG2 1BB
0115 974 2424

Capital Taxes Office,
16 Picardy Place,
Edinburgh EH1 3NB
0131 556 8511

Capital Taxes Office,
Dorchester House,
52-58 Great Victoria Street,
Belfast BT2 7BB
01232 315556

**Chartered Association of
Certified Accountants (CACA)**
29 Lincoln's Inn Fields,
London WC2A 3EE
0171 242 6855

Inland Revenue
Somerset House,
London WC2R 1LB
0171 438 6420
(or look in the phone book for
your local tax office)

**Institute of Chartered
Accountants in England and
Wales (ICAEW)**
Chartered Accountants Hall,
PO Box 433, Moorgate Place,
London EC2P 2BJ
0171 920 8100

**Institute of Chartered
Accountants in Scotland (ICAS)**
27 Queen Street,
Edinburgh EH2 1LA
0131 225 5673

TaxAid
342 Kilburn High Road,
London NW6 2QJ
0171 624 3768 (9am-11am)
(for free tax advice)

INSURANCE

**Association of British Insurers
(ABI)**
51 Gresham Street,
London EC2V 7HQ
0171 600 3333

**British Investment Insurance
Brokers Association (BIIBA)**
14 Bevis Marks,
London EC3A 7NT
0171 623 9043

**Insurance Brokers
Registration Council (IBRC)**
63 St Mary Axe,
London EC3A 8NB
0171 621 1061

Insurance Ombudsman Bureau
City Gate One, 135 Park Street,
London SE1 9EA
0171 928 4488

LAW

Law Society
113 Chancery Lane,
London WC2A 1PL
0171 242 1222

Law Society of Scotland
26 Drumsheugh Gardens,
Edinburgh EH3 7YR
0131 226 7411

Legal Services Ombudsman
22 Oxford Court,
Oxford Street,
Manchester M2 3WQ
0161 236 9532

Office for the Supervision of Solicitors
Victoria Court, 8 Dormer Place,
Leamington Spa,
Warwickshire CV32 5AE
01926 820082

CONSUMER AFFAIRS

Citizens Advice Bureau (CAB)
Myddleton House,
115-123 Pentonville Road,
London N1 9LZ
0171 833 2181 (or Yellow Pages)

Consumers' Association
2 Marylebone Road,
London NW1 4DF
0171 830 6000

Help the Aged
St James's Walk,
London EC1R 0BE
0171 253 0253

Money Advice Association
1st Floor, Gresham House,
24 Holborn Viaduct,
London EC1A 2BN
0171 236 3566

National Debtline
318 Summer Lane,
Birmingham B19 3RL
0121 359 8501

National Gas Consumers Council
6th Floor, Abford House,
15 Wilton Road,
London SW1V 1LT
0171 931 0977

Office of Electricity Regulation (OFFER)
Hagley House,
Hagley Road,
Edgbaston B16 8QG
0121 456 2100

Office of Fair Trading (OFT)
Field House,
15-25 Bream's Buildings,
London EC4A 1PR
0345 224499

Office of Gas Supply (OFGAS)
130 Wilton Road,
London SW1V 1LQ
0171 828 0898

Office of Telecommunications Services (OFTEL)
Export House,
50 Ludgate Hill,
London EC4M 7JJ
0171 822 1650

Office of Water Services (OFWAT)
Centre City Tower,
7 Hill Street,
Birmingham B5 4UA
0121 625 1300

Trading Standards Coordinating Body
PO Box 6, Fell Road,
Croydon
CR9 1LG
0181 688 1996
(or look in the phone book for your local office)

BENEFITS

Age Concern
Astral House,
1268 London Road,
London SW16 4ER
0181 679 8000
(or look in the phone book for your local office)

Benefits Agency
For advice on most social security benefits look for your local office in the phone book under Benefits Agency or Social Security

Disability Benefits
The Benefit Enquiry Line is open for people with disabilities and their carers
0800 882200

National Association for Widows
54-57 Allison Street,
Digbeth,
Birmingham B5 5TH
0121 643 8348

Office of Social Security Commissioners
83-86 Farringdon Street,
London EC4A 1PR
0171 353 5145

CHARITY

Charities Aid Foundation (CAF)
Kings Hill,
West Malling,
Kent ME19 4TA.
01732 520000

191

Index